D1074834

To Mrs. Elmer T. Anderson,
With loving kindest wishes from.
Sarah & Harry Brereton.

May 1944.

The Lost Treasures of London

When wastefull warre shall Statues over-turne,
And broiles roote out the worke of masonry
Shakespeare

Books by William Kent

London for Everyman

Dickens and Religion

London for Heretics

The George Inn, Southwark

London for Shakespeare Lovers

London for Dickens Lovers

The Testament of a Victorian Youth

London Worthies

London for the Curious

Fifty Years a Cricket Watcher

Lift up Your Heads: An Anthology for Freethinkers

Editor of

London: an Encyclopaedia

The high altar of St. Paul's Cathedral, October, 1940

William Kent

The Lost Treasures

of

London

With an Introduction by
Norman Brett-James, M.A., B.Litt., F.S.A.

London · 1947

Phoenix House Limited

Contents

The Plates

vi

The Maps

Introduction

Norman G. Brett-James, M.A., B.Litt., F.S.A.

(*Chairman and Editor of the London and Middlesex Archaeological Society*)

LONDON has faced widespread disaster and destruction twice in historic times before. The first was wilful, the second accidental. It is difficult to find any excuse for the destruction, as well as the dissolution, of the city monasteries that almost surrounded medieval London with glorious buildings and well-tended open spaces.

A great chance of utilizing both for planning a new and better London was deliberately thrown away in the middle of the sixteenth century. Opinion will always be divided as to whether an equally fine chance was forfeited more than a century later after the Great Fire of London, when the plans produced by Wren and Evelyn, by Hooke, by Newcourt and by Valentine Knight were all discarded because they seemed to the authorities and citizens far too drastic in their complete ignoring of existing shreds and frontages, and because they might have delayed the essential rebuilding of London for a decade or two.

Since that time London has grown spasmodically, with no connected plan for the place as a whole, with admirable planning in the west and south-western areas, and higgledy-piggledy building of the most haphazard kind in far too many of the poorer quarters. As a rule the more squalid the development the fewer the open spaces to compensate.

One of the aims of the planners of a new and better London is to revive local patriotism on a small scale as well as to encourage pride in London as a whole.

It is a commonplace that London means different things to different people. Speaking in an age when the great metropolis was less than one-twelfth of its present vastness, Boswell commented on several aspects of its adjacent suburbs. It was to the politician the seat of government; to the grazier an emporium for cattle; to the business man a money market; to the dramatist the home of the theatre; to the man of pleasure a place of taverns. But to the intellectual man, including presumably both Boswell and Johnson, London implied the whole of human life in all its variety.

In all ages Londoners have loved London, from the day when Dunbar called it 'the flower of cities all'. Into this well-loved London came the organized attacks from the air which the Germans who planned them hoped would—as their broadcasts threatened—destroy every vestige of the greatest city in the world.

We remember the prophecies of writers in the past who seem to have anticipated the smashing of London. Horace Walpole visualized a traveller from Lima describing the ruins of St. Paul's. Shelley looked forward to a day when 'St. Pauls and Westminster Abbey shall stand, shapeless and nameless ruins in the midst of an unpeopled marsh; when the piers of Westminster Bridge shall become the nucleus of islets of reeds and osiers and cast the jagged shadows of their broken arches on the solitary stream'. It really did seem as if Macaulay's prophecy would come true when he wrote of the traveller from New Zealand who 'shall take his stand on the broken arch of London Bridge to sketch the ruins of St. Paul's'.

Westminster has suffered severely but sporadically, and St. Paul's was within an ace of complete destruction. The Abbey had damage which was exasperating but not extensive, whereas the Deanery and the School were rendered almost uninhabitable. It was a pathetic story which the late Dean, Dr. Labilliere, had to tell, when he viewed the ruins of his deanery, and said: 'I must be the only Dean in all history who has neither Bible nor prayer-book.'

The bombs were not confined to any one area, though perhaps the regions nearest the Docks suffered most. The West End shared the destruction meted out to the East End, which fact did at least provide a common bond for all Londoners.

The clearing away of the damaged buildings and the digging down to their foundations have given us glimpses of an unknown London. To stand in Fetter Lane and to look east and north-east is to realize to-day that there is a definite Fleet River valley between Holborn Hill and Snow Hill, and to re-capture something of what our great grandparents knew before Holborn Viaduct was built.

Everyone, no doubt, has his own special bit of London, whose loss he deplores. Mine is Gray's Inn, which lost hall, chapel and library, or most of them.

But we need a clear, succinct account of all the damage which has befallen Central London, and there are few who can compete with William Kent as a chronicler of the London we have lost. He has a very well deserved reputation for such work, based on a lifetime in London and constant research into its story. He has compiled volumes to suit different tastes—*London for Shakespeare Lovers, London for Dickens Lovers, London for Heretics, London for Everyman;* and he has done honour to many past and a few present citizens of the Metropolis in his *London Worthies*. He has provided a reference volume in his *Encyclopaedia of London*, and he knows the London of Charles Lamb as well as anyone else, though he has not yet written a book on the subject. He might with ample justice quote Charles Dickens's remark and apply it to himself—'I suppose myself to know this rather large city as well as anyone in it,' and there would be few to challenge William Kent's claim. if he cared to make it.

Preface

THIS is a sad book. It cannot be otherwise. It is bound to wring the withers of the Londoners who, having for five years bent a keen eye on vacancy, in the phrase of Johnson about Boswell's antiquarian ardour, have become hardened to the sight of ruin. It may be still sadder to the visitor from the country or from overseas who recalls the City he once knew and perhaps made his home and who has, by means of piecemeal press news, been able only to guess at its suffering.

If while much has been taken much abides, there is no denying that our losses have been severe. Nineteen churches (sixteen of them Wren's) in the square mile of the City have been reduced to shells. Still worse has been the fate of the Halls of the City Companies. Of thirty-four standing at the commencement of the War, only three are undamaged—the Apothecaries' (Blackfriars Lane), the Ironmongers' (Shaftesbury Place, Aldersgate Street), and the Vintners' (Upper Thames Street). Most of the others will have to be rebuilt. It is appropriate that the Ironmongers' Company should have escaped this time, as their Hall was the only one to suffer in the War of 1914-18.

We all have our own personal sense of loss, apart from the human bereavement which has, unhappily, been the lot of many. I recall that my late friend, Read (many years ago a colleague in the Solicitor's Department of the L.C.C.), was much saddened by the destruction of the Church of St. Lawrence Jewry, which he had, a few weeks before, shown to a party, including myself. This sorrow was not entirely due to the loss of its architectural beauties. He told me that his mother had taken her first communion there. I have the keenest pangs when in the Temple or where Paternoster Row used to be. My career started with books (in the warehouse of Hutchinson and Company) and concluded in 'the valley of the shadow of the law'. Briefs, however, have but a brief interest for any one; books remain influences for life. Such a holocaust of books has never before been known in this country. In a very small circle, of which the diameter line was represented by the west side of Paternoster Row, in one night—that of the last Sunday of 1940—there went to the flames about five million books, considerably more than the whole of those in the British Museum.

After such losses as these, it is small consolation to note the singular immunity of places of entertainment. Hardly any of the theatres were destroyed, and our principal hostelries—the George Inn in Southwark, the Cock, and

Cheshire Cheese in Fleet Street—survive almost unimpaired. More remarkable, and a source of more satisfaction, for they were recognizable military objectives, was the survival of the bridges. Temporary bridges were half completed between Vauxhall and Westminster, and between Westminster and Charing Cross, but were happily never required. A crater was made on the south side of Lambeth Bridge but caused no inconvenience. It was curious that the only bridge that had to be closed for any time was the notorious one at Charing Cross. If the spirit of that great London-lover John Burns could be summoned up and again command its vibrant physical voice, it might be imagined as protesting that Hungerford Bridge had not been bombed enough. If only it had fallen into the river, he would have said, we might have seen the last of this horrible abortion of Father Thames. I know he wished that Mr. Herbert Morrison could have used some of the zeal he displayed in demolishing the bridge at Waterloo in performing a similar office for its shabby neighbour.

Where can consolation be found? In the large amount of plate that all the Companies and the churches seem carefully to have guarded? This only suggests much else that might well have been saved. With a little more trouble we might still have the crossed-legged knights in the Temple Church. London's 'piled stones' are rich with memories of the past for some of us; we hug our books—our Stow, our County history, our volumes of the Royal Commission—and garner up memories in our minds, aided by their pictures, of what we can never again behold.

Yet something remains for gratitude. We have not been exiled from what Lamb called the Old Jerusalem. We have not raised our sad and wistful songs on the banks of the Rhine, like the Israelites by the waters of Babylon. We have not seen the ruins of St. Paul's Cathedral, nor yet a broken arch of London Bridge. Westminster Abbey, probably the most precious pile to all London-lovers, is almost unimpaired. We still have the churches of St. Bartholomew-the-Great and of St. Helen, Bishopsgate, whose preservation might most devoutly have been desired.

After Dr. Johnson had surveyed the ruins of St. Andrew's Cathedral, caused by another fanatic, John Knox, Boswell mentioned dinner. 'Ay, ay, sir,' said the Doctor, 'amid all these sorrowful scenes, I have no objection to dinner.' Our present meagre rationing might not have taken off the edge of the Doctor's wrath, but we can say to one another with the utmost sincerity that it might have been worse, and most of us expected that it would be.

Recently, in pursuance of a literary commission, I had occasion to traverse the columns of *The Times* in 1938 and 1939. What dismal forebodings I found as the war cloud grew bigger on the horizon! One then envisaged bombs persistent and plentiful, day after day, week after week, like the rain that fell in Noah's flood. It was bad enough, I admit, but who, in September 1939, anticipating a war that was to last five and a half years, would not have predicted far worse things? One writer, referring to the most devastated area in London —that between Aldersgate Street and Moorgate—likened it to Pompeii. Only a super-optimist, qualified for a Tapley gold medal, would have denied the probability of this being the state of the whole city after so long a conflict.

Indeed, it might have been much worse. Few people take any notice of the inscriptions on the Monument—quite untouched by the blitz. There it is recorded that, in the Great Fire of 1666, London lost 89 churches, 13,200 houses, and 400 streets. Of 26 wards of the City, 15 were utterly destroyed, and 8 were half burnt. Leake's map, made after the Fire, shows London almost entirely cleared by the burning, the one immune spot being at the north-east corner of the City. Yet London rose again, as it will for the sight of our children or, at any rate, our grandchildren. The blitz will become the modern landmark of London history in modern times, as was the Great Fire of 1666 in the pre-War era.

I am glad, too, to think that there is now a more genuine love of London, its history, and its treasures than ever before. Supposing that, after the Great Fire, there had been formed a procession of mourning for London's great losses. Who would have been there? No doubt Charles II and James, Duke of York; perhaps Samuel Pepys, John Evelyn, Robert Hooke, Sir Christopher Wren, and a few members of the Society of Antiquaries. To-day, there would be vastly more. Members of the London and Middlesex Archaeological Society (approaching its centenary), such as its able and learned Chairman and Editor, Norman G. Brett-James, who has produced a monumental work *The Growth of Stuart London*. There would also be its enthusiastic Secretary, Commander Bridgmore Brown (whose stimulus helped to produce this book), Mr. Allen Walker (the mentor of my young days), and Mr. Francis R. Taylor, an enthusiastic photographer who did much work for the Royal Commission. Prominent in the Ecclesiological Society's contingent would be Mr. Edward Yates, who has a collection of lantern slides numbering 35,000—perhaps a world-record. Once asked to lend a few slides on fonts, he promptly replied that he could oblige with 600! Then there would be representatives of the London Society, of the London Appreciation Society (H. L. Bryant Peers and H. T. Phippard), and of the London Explorers, led by the enthusiastic and irrepressible William Margrie.

In the seventeenth century many men and women, in the state of life into which it had pleased the Fates to call them, were incapable of appreciating London's architectural, artistic, and antiquarian treasures. How could they peruse monuments when they could not pen their own names? Osbert Lancaster in *The Listener* said: 'It must be admitted that for 99.9 per cent of the public the grief felt for any individual architectural casualty is largely esoteric; such losses fall into the same category as the death of poor Aunt

3

Agatha, whom the family had always referred to with deepest affection, but no one had ever actually seen.' I agree that people have mourned the loss of buildings they have never troubled to enter but, when I recall those who, faint yet pursuing, have traipsed after me, in fair and foul weather, in the course of my thirty years and more as a London guide, I feel this figure is too high.

They have had little encouragement from their political leaders. The latter can perorate about London, but do they perambulate its streets, as John Burns loved to do? He has been without a peer in this regard and perhaps, since the Reform Bill (to go no further back) the only prominent politician to study its history and antiquity. One of the most sapient remarks ever made by Samuel Johnson was that no man was a hypocrite in his pleasures. Those of Burns (as my biography of him will show), included buying books about London, talking about it, and conducting his friends to its show places. This, not oratory, is the evidence of sincere affection, and I am sad to reflect how little of it was displayed in high places during the recent war, when some of us tried to enlist interest in plans for showing London to the unprecedented number of men from foreign climes who walked its streets. Most of them were left to the attentions of taxi-drivers who did one good thing—they provided me with material for a book on London mythology which one day I hope to publish.

This book, as I have said, is sad in its tone for all readers; sadder for many antiquaries, for they are seldom to be found amongst the young. An interest in the past seems to come more readily to those who themselves have a long one, and an estimate of the expectation of life of the average antiquary would not be encouraging. Still, we can apply here to buildings what Tennyson said of men and women: ' 'Tis better to have loved and lost than never to have loved at all.' In our eventide, we have memory to feed upon, when we view 'bare, ruined choirs' where maybe weeds now spring. We may not see the new London, but we may see its foundations laid. The phoenix that concludes this book is prophetic; London will rise again.

Now for a few words about my objectives in this book. That it will fill a need I am convinced from remarks made by my friends who knew it was in the making. I have designed it so that it should satisfy the curiosity of anyone who wants to know what has happened to some well-known London building interesting to him. Of course, I have not catalogued all; I have chosen those of general interest. Of those of which I have made no mention, it may be assumed that they have not been damaged or that the damage sustained was trifling. I have not attempted any detailed history of the places mentioned. Anyone, like myself, who has written a number of books on London, cannot avoid a little overlapping, but it has been reduced to a minimum. This book should be a welcome supplement to my *London for*

Everyman and *Encyclopaedia of London*, the first edition of which has been exhausted for a long time.

Something must be said of the arrangement of *The Lost Treasures of London*. For the convenience of readers, the matter has been arranged in the form of Walks. It is estimated that each of these will not occupy more than two hours, at a normal pace. Those who require information about any particular thoroughfare or building can refer to the Index.

It is assumed that many readers will like to carry the book on their pilgrimages through the City. For this reason the information about a particular locality has been grouped under the title of its principal thoroughfare or a well-known building. For the benefit of visitors, guidance is given on how to find the places mentioned, and their positions in relation to each other. In addition a map has been provided for each of the Central London Walks, in which all the thoroughfares to be visited are shown, and the positions of buildings indicated. Streets to which no reference is made in the text are omitted from the maps, except in the case of main thoroughfares or those which will help the walker to find the streets in which are places he wishes to visit. As in the case of my *Encyclopaedia*, the survey is restricted to the County of London.

It remains now only to thank those who have so willingly assisted. Special acknowledgment must be made to the following:

1. For information about the churches. *Mr. J. M. Bruce-Gardyne, B.A.; the Rev. P. B. Clayton; the Rev. R. H. Couchman (also for his kindness in affording every facility for photographing his gridiron weather-vane); Mr. K. L. Davies; the Rev. J. H. Fynes-Clinton; the Rev. T. R. Hine Haycock; Capt. Owen F. Hunt, M.C.; Mr. E. J. Mander; Mr. C. G. Misselbrook; Mr. S. Hewitt Pitt; Prebendary Arthur Taylor; the Rev. O. H. Thomas.*

2. For information about the City Companies. *Mr. Roland Champness (Cutlers); Mr. John C. Druce (Innholders); Mr. Guy Eagleton (Haberdashers); Mr. W. A. D. Englefield (Painter-Stainers); Mr. L. E. L. Hall, LL.D. (Butchers); Mr. John Hingdon (Leathersellers); Mr. E. R. Hughes, C.V.O. (Goldsmiths); Mr. A. Charles Knight, J.P., F.S.A. (Barbers); Mr. E. Fairfax Lucy (Merchant Taylors); Mr. J. Curzon Mander (Cordwainers); Mr. Ernest Mills (Parish Clerks); Mr. R. H. Monier-Williams (Tallow Chandlers); Mr. W. R. Nicholls (Salters); Mr. H. C. Osborne, M.C. (Carpenters); Mr. R. A. B. Powell (Drapers); Mr. R. T. Rivington (Stationers); Mr. W. Dumville Smith (Girdlers); Mr. R. J. D. Smith (Coach and Coach-Harness Makers); Mr. W. Newcome Wright (Bakers).*

3. For information about Libraries. *Dr. Irene Churchill (Lambeth Palace); Mr. E. A. P. Hart (Inner Temple); Mr. T. Hodgkinson (Lincoln's Inn); Mr. W. Holden, M.B.E. (Gray's Inn); Mr. Raymond Smith (Guildhall); Mr. H. A. C. Sturgess (Middle Temple); Mr. John Wilkes (University College); I am also indebted for information about books to Mr. Edwin Pughe, Deputy Chairman of*

Simpkin Marshall and Co. (1941) *Ltd., and to Mr. Desmond Flower of Cassell and Co., Ltd.*

I owe grateful thanks to Mr. E. S. Underwood, F.R.I.B.A., for lending a photograph of the ruins of Christ Church, Newgate, and taking me over them, and to my friends Mr. Edward Yates and Mr. Francis Taylor (both unwithered from most strenuous antiquarian activity). Thanks are also due to the Royal Commission for permission to use some pictures from their magnificent volumes on London; to the Controller, H.M. Stationery Office; to the British Broadcasting Corporation; to Messrs B. T. Batsford, Ltd.; to the *Illustrated London News*; and to the *New York Times* and to *The Times* (London) for similar concessions. Miss K. R. Jeater of the latter paper was most kind in giving assistance. The Rev. P. B. Clayton, and the Western Union Telegraph Company, have also kindly lent blocks. In this connection, I am grateful, too, to Mr. Terence Gould, one of the Company's staff.

The National Buildings Record, the Curators of the South Kensington Museums, Mr. F. R. Doubleday of the Zoological Society and the Ministry of Works have been most helpful. I must also express my indebtedness to the *City Press*, founded in 1857. It is invaluable to students of Old London.

I am grateful to Mr. Harold Adshead for permission to use his charming poems. These have also appeared in *World Digest*, so a further acknowledgment is due to the editor of that journal. The poem by my old friend McNulty on flowers in the city I am also pleased to be able to use.

I am obliged for help given by old friends like Mr. P. W. Bennett, Mr. J. R. Chinnery, Ernest Waters, and Mr. F. Woodward. The last-mentioned, by the time this book appears, will have ceased to act as a delightful guide at Lambeth Palace. Miss L. Mont-Clar has given valuable assistance in checking my MS. Sir Bryan Fell, K.C., M.C., C.B., has kindly allowed me to quote from his most admirable book *The Houses of Parliament*. To Ernest Benn, Ltd., I am grateful for permission to quote from *Fleet Street Blitzkrieg Diary* by Gordon Robbins. Useful volumes have been *Historic London under Fire* (Ecclesiological Society); *A Literary Journey Through War-Time Britain* by A. C. Ward (published, so far, only in New York); the volumes of the Royal Commission; *The Bombed Buildings of Britain* (published by the Architectural Press, with valuable notes by John Summerson); the *Evening News* volume *Hitler Passed This Way*. Articles in *The Times* have been most informative.

Those concerned about the future of London and the question of the City churches would be interested in the able book *How Shall We Re-plan London?* by my old friend, C. B. Purdom (1945); also in *Bombed Churches as War Memorials* (Architectural Press).

In this connection it is interesting to mention that, in the rebuilding, the

City may become more residential. Today residents are less than five thous-
and. There have been for about twenty years modern flats in Crane Court,
Fleet Street, and a building has recently been requisitioned in Botolph Lane
to accommodate residents.

W.K.
April 1946

The Air Raids In General

LONDON, like the rest of the country, had a long lull before the storm. On 3rd September 1939 at 11.15 a.m., almost as soon as the Rt. Hon. Neville Chamberlain, the Prime Minister, had finished his broadcast announcing a state of war between Great Britain and the German Reich, there was a short air raid warning. It was a false alarm. The following night there was a warning from 1.30 to 4.30 a.m. but nothing of the enemy was heard. On 5th September there was another from 7 to 9 a.m. There were further warnings in Kent during September, but no more in London until 25th June 1940.

For six weeks after this, news came of raids far afield: early in July the north-east of England and Scotland were attacked; in a Scottish town eleven were killed. Then the raiders appeared over the south coast. On 11th July, twenty-two were shot down; on 29th July twenty were destroyed in the neighbourhood of Dover. The bag on 8th August numbered fifty-three—over the English Channel; on 11th August this was increased to sixty; on 12th August thirty-nine were brought down over the Isle of Wight and Portsmouth, and fifty-nine over the south coast on 13th August.

The raiders came nearer London. On 16th August they were over Hertfordshire, Essex and Surrey, and a number of deaths were reported. On 18th August there were two warnings in South London; on 23rd August the raiders were over the outskirts, and two cinemas, a branch bank, and a number of houses were destroyed.

On the night of Saturday, 24th August 1940, the first bombs fell in the City. It was remarkable that the area visited was approximately that where the first Zeppelin raid took place. Michael MacDonagh (*In London During the Great War*, 1935) described his experience on 9th September 1915:

I was writing in my study about twenty minutes to eleven o'clock when the roar of bombs and guns broke upon my meditations and, stepping out upon a little balcony of the room at the back of the house, commanding a wide sweep of the sky north-east, I saw an amazing spectacle. High in the sky was a Zeppelin picked out of the darkness by searchlights—a long narrow object of a silvery hue! I felt like what a watcher of the skies must feel when a new planet swims into his ken. For it was my first sight of an enemy airship!

The raider was striking at the very heart of London—in the City between St. Paul's Cathedral and the Mansion House and the Bank. This I found when I went out this morning to see the effects of the bombardment. In Wood Street and Silver Street behind Cheapside and quite close to Guildhall, there were gutted and smouldering warehouses, some other premises less damaged, and there were deep holes in the road-

8

ways. . . . Making my way across Moorgate Street and down London Wall, I came to the place where a bomb dropped in front of a motor omnibus bound for Liverpool Street Station, and blew it to pieces. Twenty people were on board, including the driver and conductor. Nine were instantly killed, and eleven seriously injured. The driver had both his legs blown off and died on his way to hospital. The door of a block of offices was pointed out to me where the housekeeper standing on the steps was killed. The roadway was strewn with the glass of shattered windows. Entering Liverpool Street Station, I saw a section of the permanent way that was wrecked by a bomb. The same raider dropped a bomb in Bartholomew Close, which smashed the windows of Bart's Hospital and narrowly missed the ancient church of St. Bartholomew-the-Great.

There was a much milder commencement of the attack on civilians, destined to be vastly more deadly, in the second European war. It was reported that only four people were killed in the first raid; they were not in the City. The buildings destroyed in the Cripplegate area were mostly millinery and gown warehouses. For a fortnight thereafter there was little worthy of note in the London district. Then, on a fine Saturday afternoon, 7th September 1940, waves of planes came over flying eastwards. For some hours there was a tremendous attack upon the Docks by German bombers, with a crew of four or five, escorted by half a dozen fighters. There was a terrible amount of devastation amongst the small houses in the borough of Stepney. An East End doctor said that no area of fifty square yards remained untouched. There were brought into action 2,000 firemen and 3,000 pumps.

The attempt to disrupt commerce did not succeed, and there was small damage caused to food in the Docks. Of course, thousands were made homeless. There followed what was described as 'a miniature Dunkirk'. Two thousand refugees were evacuated by pleasure steamers. 'Little boats of the River Emergency Service which in peace-time took holiday makers to Margate and Southend and ran "bob" trips down the river, were seen chugging along the riverside wharves and jetties, defying high explosive and incendiary bombs, walls of flame, and clouds of choking fumes. . . . With a few bundles of clothes the refugees climbed aboard and were taken by river to the safety zone or ferried across to the opposite bank.' (*News Chronicle*.)

The late John Burns told the present writer that, when he witnessed the attack upon the Docks from the roof of the National Liberal Club, he was reminded of Daniell's picture *The Destruction of Jerusalem*.

On the next night there was another severe raid. There was a warning at about 8 o'clock, and the 'All Clear' was not sounded until 5 o'clock the next morning. Thereafter there was to be no intermission for weeks. On 12th September St. Thomas's Hospital was hit for the first time; on the same night a delayed action bomb fell outside St. Paul's Cathedral; on 14th September Buckingham Palace was struck; on 15th September there was a crater in the

Strand outside Somerset House; on 16th September the West End was attacked—in the neighbourhood of Bruton Street. On most nights the City was under warning as long as the hours of darkness. Before the end of the month the Church of St. Clement Danes, Strand, had been gutted, and bombs had been dropped on Lambeth Palace. Other buildings damaged at this time were Guy's Hospital, the Tate Gallery, and the office of *The Times* in Queen Victoria Street. In October there was no improvement except in the diminution of day raids. The reredos of St. Paul's Cathedral was destroyed; there was damage to St. James's Church, Piccadilly, more damage to Lambeth Palace, the Tate Gallery, and St. Thomas's Hospital. There was a warning every October night. Not until Sunday, 7th November, after fifty-seven nights in succession, was there an interval. Rough weather for a week brought this about. On the night of 19th November there was a heavy raid. When, about this time, the Southern Railway warehouse at Blackfriars was hit, it cost *The Times* seven weeks' supply of newsprint.

Londoners, for many weeks, lived a more hectic life than any of their forebears had ever experienced. No comparison could fitly be made with other times when advancing war had threatened its inhabitants. In 1588 the approach of the Spanish Armada sent Queen Elizabeth to Tilbury to rally her troops. In 1642 the Royalist forces reached Brentford. In 1745 there was trepidation because the army of the 'Young Pretender' had, in its southward march, swiftly reached Derby. These alarms were trifles compared with the Zeppelins that came between 1915 and 1918, but they, in their turn, hardly counted as a menace compared with the extent of the aerial invasion of September 1940. In the first World War raids were intermittent and short: in the second War for many weeks they were continuous and long. For night after night in September and October 1940 the warning was in operation for hours on end, sometimes from dusk to dawn.

Daylight terrors, for a few weeks, vied with those of darkness. Workers on their way to factory and office might be held up for hours in tube or shelter. At the other end of the day they might be still far from home when the woeful wailing indicated that the nightly visitation had already come. Some, when they reached home, ensconced themselves under a strong table or in a cellar; only the bolder spirits slept on an upper floor. Then, as it was evident the raids were to be the regular routine of war and not merely an episode, safer shelter was sought. The tubes were invaded as affording good protection. At first their use was forbidden, but mass action forced the London Passenger Transport Board to permit entry, and nightly long queues waited for that admission which for them meant safety. They slept on the stairs, on the motionless escalators, and in passages. Those who had before supposed that sleep would never be successfully wooed save in a comfortable bed, worn out by work and worry secured some kind of repose in this way. Later the

Board did much to make the shelterers more comfortable. Sometimes, in the early days of the blitz, as early as noon a queue could be seen at a tube station awaiting entry to secure a place for the night. In due course the issue of tickets prevented this wasteful consumption of time. Some old people, while the daylight raids were still a terror, lived underground, and saw less of the sky than any miner. Shelters were opened everywhere, and the present writer had some experience of a typical one beneath Thames House, a huge structure on Millbank, Westminster. Here, nightly, a thousand people gathered, a mass of congested humanity lying closer together than the dead in any graveyard. Most of them had but a rug, as a substitute for a mattress, or a cushion, just to keep the hips from painful contact with the hard floor. Yet they were comparatively happy in their rest knowing that by the sacrifice of so much comfort they had at least obtained security.

A popular shelter was the crypt of the Church of St. Martin-in-the-Fields, Trafalgar Square. Here a place could be secured by depositing some luggage on the spot the prospective lodger proposed to occupy. Points to be considered were the absence of draught, and the presence of sufficient light for reading. At night it was indeed, as one writer called it, 'St. Martin's among the Tombstones'. More than a hundred people were huddled up on the spacious floor of the crypt; the living had sought shelter amongst the dead. Happily the church sustained no damage, though one night a piece of the railing was blown away by a bomb. A woman had been standing close by, at the bus stop. She was urged to go into the church for safety, but she replied that she was anxious to get home. A few seconds later she was killed. One night bombs fell on the escalator of Trafalgar Square Station and in the Adelphi. There was momentarily a disposition to panic: the bombs sounded nearer than they were. The provision of shelters and amenities for the shelterers was a good work, but a little marred by that disposition to Draconian severity which, said Lord Salisbury, sometimes accompanies philanthropic legislation. At an unconscionably early hour a policewoman roused the sleepers and bade them go about their business.

The high-light of tragedy was on the bombing, but fatalities incidental to it were many, and little known. A man who had been bombed at his office and bombed at his house, went into the garden and cut his throat with a carving knife. Another, bombed at business and distraught by the difficulty of travelling to it, took spirits of salt in the basement of his premises. A third, finding sleep impossible under the noise and stress of the raids, returned to the house he had evacuated and there gassed himself. A child hearing the siren, rushed across the road and was killed by a bus.

The black-out made London indeed a city of dreadful night, and street fatalities in September and October 1940 increased at least fourfold. At one inquest it was shown that in Hampstead Road a body must have been carried under the front valance of a bus for 125 yards. It was in such a mangled condition that the brother of the deceased could identify it only by clothing and correspondence. In the north of London a bus collided with a lorry and caught fire through the exuding petrol. Amongst the passengers was a soldier who was so badly burnt that he was identified only by his spectacles, his cigarette case, and a camp bed he was known to have been carrying. There were other tragedies, but they too paled into insignificance beside those caused by the terror from the air. At a cross-roads at Wimbledon, in October 1940, a family of four in a motor-car were killed by collision with a bus, but there was no mention of this catastrophe in the press. London supped full with horrors, and there was no need to titillate the appetite with such trifles as these.

There were aspects of humour even in all this sadness. Life became a bit chaotic in the best regulated offices. There were alarms in rumour, alarms in fact, and certainly alarms of convenience. Never had the habitually slothful faced what that medieval civil servant Geoffrey Chaucer might have called 'Ye Book of Ye Tardy Comer' with such assurance! Under the heading 'Reason for late attendance', a witty legal colleague of the writer at County Hall had in peace-time made such entries as 'A damned good one', 'Domestic Staff failed to report for duty', and 'Pipped by a minute—physic'. Inventiveness of this kind was no longer called for. 'Delayed by air raid' not only justified itself by assonance, it covered a multitude of personal shortcomings. If you were missing at the other end of the day, Charles Lamb's excuse that if you came late you atoned by going early, was not very wide of the mark.

In the autumn of 1940 there was an action fixed for hearing at Clerkenwell County Court arising out of an accident in Holloway Road in respect of which a woman sued the London Passenger Transport Board for damages. On the day in question the Board's Counsel, Mr. R. T. Monier-Williams (the grandson of a famous Oriental scholar, and an able barrister, much liked in the profession) did not appear. In due course came a message to the effect that he had no trousers, in fact hardly a rag of clothing, through his Kensington residence having been bombed. The present writer, who was deputed to instruct him, found a substitute in the Robing Room of the Court. The case was not reached, and was adjourned to a date about a month later. On that day it was again not heard, although the Plaintiff had travelled from Sheffield, to which town she had removed from the terrors of London life. On the third occasion, when the case was called it was announced that the Plaintiff had not arrived. It was explained to the Judge that it had been ascertained that she had left Sheffield by the night train, and that the train was nearing London. It was agreed therefore to hear her witness in the hope that, by the time she had left the box, the Plaintiff would appear. The hope was vain, so the Judge adjourned for a few hours. He was asked to return to court when he was informed that the Plaintiff was not on that train. She had started for the station at Sheffield, but had been compelled to return to her home because of a raid there. On the fourth occasion the Plaintiff did reach the Court. She gave evidence, and heard the Judge sum up against her and give judgment for the Board!

No doubt volumes could be compiled of such odd happenings; the dislocation of business, the minor hardships of life (often for an area of a mile or so after a raid, no hot drink could be obtained in a restaurant for want of gas) consequent on the air-raids.

There were reported moving incidents by flood and field. A large trench shelter in Kennington Park was hit, causing a terrible number of casualties. A water-main burst at Balham and this led to the drowning of about 68 shelterers. On Sunday, 12th December, came one of the fiercest attacks. There were heavy bombs dropped in New Bridge Street and the Temple; many fires were caused south of the river. For three days at Christmas there was a welcome lull. It was followed by something worse than had hitherto been experienced.

There may have been worse nights—two possible ones will be mentioned —but few Londoners had a more memorable experience than on Sunday, 29th December 1940. The warning sounded at 6.10 p.m. and, in less than a quarter of an hour, there was a fall of incendiary bombs quite unprecedented. They were weird and terrifying. They made hardly as much noise as heavy rain; there was practically no sound of concussion but they caused conflagration everywhere. The City was lit up as it never could have been since the Great Fire of 1666. Anyone wanting to describe it might well have borrowed a passage from the Diary of Samuel Pepys:

. . . . *saw the fire grow; and as it grew darker, appeared more and more, and in corners and upon steeples, and between churches and houses, as far as we could see up the hill of the City in a most horrid, malicious, bloody flame, not like the fine flame of an ordinary fire.* (2nd Sept., 1666.)

It was on this awful night that so many of the City churches were practically destroyed. Also, there were lost in millions, books from the region of Paternoster Row; literary losses far exceeding those of the stationers who, in 1666, stuffed their valuables in the Chapel of St. Faith under St. Paul's Cathedral. The bombs came down from 'Molotov bread baskets', fifty or a hundred at a time. There were some high-explosive bombs (one killed eighty horses in a brewery) but it appeared that a second invasion with a load of these was frustrated by a change of weather. This may well have been, for the 'All Clear' came before midnight, unexpectedly early. So the New Year made a cheerless start. For several days there was no electricity in parts of the City. There were great gaps in Cheapside and widespread devastation in the neighbourhood of Cripplegate.

In January 1941 there were three quiet nights in one week, but on the 11th there was another fire-raising raid; bombs fell in Mitre Court, Fleet Street, and in Gray's Inn Road. After the third week there was something of a lull for about a month. This was probably due to bad weather. The raiding recommenced on 21st February and there were some serious 'incidents' in March, when Liverpool Street Station, the Law Courts, once again the Temple, and Serjeants' Inn were affected.

On 16th April came what the Germans maintained was the 'greatest air-raid of all time' on London. It was claimed by the Germans that 100,000 bombs were dropped. It was on this occasion that the churches of St. Andrew, Holborn, and the adjacent City Temple were burnt out. Fleet Street escaped, but the Holborn area suffered much damage, as did Oxford Street and some of the suburbs, Chelsea Old Church being destroyed. Traffic was stopped in the Strand; several railway termini were out of action; the District Railway was affected; and transit was further impeded by unexploded bombs in Queen Victoria Street, Cheapside, and Ludgate Hill. Bombers were brought down in Campden Hill Road, Kensington, and at Wimbledon.

It is appropriate to mention that a few hours before this raid the north tower of the Crystal Palace (280 feet high) had been blown up by dynamite in ten seconds by Walter Couzens of Rochester, who had forty years' experience in this line. It was said that the tower was a landmark for enemy raiders. At any rate it provided 840 tons of metal—a contrast to the contribution of the louse (see p. 106).

There was another raid, but not so intensive, on Saturday, 19th April. Bombs fell in Kingsway and in Southwark Street. Perhaps the heaviest was the raid on Saturday, 10th May 1940. On this night the Church of St. Clement Danes received its knock-out blow; Serjeants' Inn was destroyed; also the Mercers' Hall in Cheapside. The House of Commons Chamber was reduced to a shell and Big Ben was hit, though it did not stop. Charterhouse was badly damaged; the Deanery of Westminster Abbey was burnt out; the British Museum was affected; Lambeth Palace had its hottest night. The area round the Tower of London was again visited; the churches of St. Olave, Hart Street (famous for its Pepys associations) and All Hallows, Barking, were reduced to shells. The smell of burning was never so pronounced in London as on that Sunday morning; a pall of smoke over the City seemed to symbolize its sense of mourning.

Those who walked about the street that day would have been more cheerful had they known that this so ruthless raid was to be the last formidable one. There followed a lull for three weeks. On Whit Sunday, 1941, there was a three hours' warning but no sound of bombs. The invasion of Russia that commenced in the same month brought a very long lull.

Afterwards, at long intervals, there were raids, but rarely over central

London. There was a brief recurrence there at the beginning of 1944, when a few bombs again fell in Fleet Street; one damaged the Church of St. Dunstan-in-the-West.

On Tuesday, 13th June 1944, came the first flying bomb. It landed near Bow Station, in the east of London. It was not understood at the time, and it was given out that an aircraft had fallen, but the crew could not be found. The flying bombs came in force on the night of Thursday, 15th June. The present writer was on fire-watch duty, and well recalls the mystification about what was going on. The warning came soon after eleven. Hour after hour went by with no 'All Clear' signal, though for long this had come within an hour or two. Watchers occasionally saw lights travelling rapidly through the sky and then disappear suddenly from view. It was not until after nine next morning that the 'All Clear' signal came. It was the longest warning since May 1941.

For about three months there was no cessation. It was a repetition of the early days of the blitz, when there were daylight raids, but in a worse form. Then there were sometimes fairly long intervals of peace. Now, at any rate, in South London, intervals were rare and short. On some days it was 'All Clear' for not more than half an hour or so at any one time. Shopping was a hazardous occupation, and at New Cross, one Saturday morning, over a hundred were killed in a Woolworth's stores. The Borough of Lewisham suffered most from the flying bombs; next came Wandsworth. The bombs seemed to come regularly at an hour when most people were leaving for work or returning from it. Londoners had to carry on bravely in defiance of threatened death from the skies at any moment. It was now that the surface shelters, little used hitherto, came into full occupation, and proved their worth. By day neighbourliness grew apace as the inhabitants of a street rushed in and out of a shelter from morning to evening. At night its dark recesses were filled with sleepers, lying almost completely dressed in the bunks, who became inured to a lack of privacy which they had never before experienced.

Flying bombs disturbed the usual placidity of Lord's Cricket Ground, St. John's Wood, on two occasions. First on Saturday, 29th July 1944, when Lieut. J. D. Robertson (Middlesex) and Sergeant C. B. Harris (Notts.) were batting for the Army against the Royal Air Force. All the players and the two umpires fell flat on the turf. No one was badly shaken as the bomb dropped in Regent's Park. Secondly, on Friday, 11th August 1944, when the match was Lord's XI v. Public Schools. *Wisden's Cricketers' Almanac* (1945) says: 'During the first innings a flying bomb exploded less than 200 yards from Lord's. Pieces of soil fell on the pitch, but the players, particularly the boys, most of whom had never experienced such an attack, stopped only while the bomb was seen hurtling down. The break in the game lasted little more than half a minute, and the spectators, some of whom had thrown themselves flat under seats for protection, showed their appreciation of the boys' pluck with hearty hand-claps.'

The flying bombs came far more to the suburbs than to central London. One of the few that fell in the City damaged the Butchers' Hall in Bartholomew Close and, very slightly, the neighbouring Church of St. Bartholomew-the-Great. Another practically destroyed the charming Staple Inn which is just outside the City boundary. In Westminster the destruction of the Guards' Chapel, described elsewhere (see p. 118), was a most serious catastrophe. A flying bomb that dropped in Aldwych about midday caused many casualties.

By the beginning of September 1944, when the first V2 rocket arrived, the flying-bomb attacks had become more intermittent. They continued, however, at intervals until March 1945.

The first V2 fell at Chiswick on the night of Friday, 8th September 1944. The loud report was plainly heard at Westminster. This projectile travelled at 3,000 miles an hour.

Possibly one rocket fell within the City, at the corner of Farringdon Road and Charterhouse Street, which is on the border line of the City of London, the Borough of Holborn and the Borough of Finsbury. This occurred at about noon on 8th March 1945; over a hundred people were killed. Almost the last rocket destroyed Whitefield's Tabernacle, Tottenham Court Road. The very last explosive to fall anywhere in London was the rocket that descended on 27th March 1945 at 7.20 a.m. It hit two blocks of flats at Hughes Mansions, Stepney, killing 134 people. The last to fall in England dropped the same day at 4.54 p.m. on Court Road, Orpington. The number of rockets that reached Britain was 1,050; 2,754 people were killed, and 6,523 seriously injured.

The City's blitz record was published towards the end of February 1944. It was as follows: Out of the total of 460 acres of built-up land in the City, buildings covering about 164 acres were destroyed. The sirens sounded 715 times, 415 warnings being given during the last five months of 1940. A total of nine weeks had been spent under air-raid 'alert' conditions. High-explosive bombs of varying sizes numbering 417 were dropped in the City, together with 13 parachute mines, 2,498 oil bombs, and many thousands of incendiaries. Some 1,300 incidents were reported to the Report and Control Centre; 183 of these were between 6.20 p.m. and 11.40 p.m. on 29th December 1940. The number of killed then was slightly over 200; 363 were seriously injured. On the night of 10-11th January 1941, 111 persons were killed and 433 injured at the Bank tube station, in Liverpool Street, and in Cheapside. Only the rocket at Stepney caused any serious addition to these figures.

The following are particulars of the warnings given over an area approximating to the County of London: 1939—3; 1940—417; 1941—154; 1942—25; 1943—95; 1944—508; 1945—22: total, 1,224.

Walk 1

*Strand ★ The Temple ★ Lincoln's Inn ★ Fleet Street
Ludgate Hill ★ St. Paul's Cathedral ★ Paternoster Row ★
Cannon Street ★ London Bridge ★ Southwark*

STRAND

THERE has been little damage to the main thoroughfare. In Adam Street, on the south side, there remains one house (No. 7), similar to those erected by the Adam brothers on Adelphi Terrace. There has also survived Sir James Barrie's flat in Robert Street.

On the west side of Adam Street is John Street. Here is the SOCIETY OF ARTS HALL. It was built by the Adam brothers in 1772-4. James Barry, R.A., covered the walls with pictures under the general title *Human Culture*. One of these included figures of William Penn, Edmund Burke, Dr. Johnson, and Dr. Burney. The Hall has suffered from bombs, but not very seriously. Part of the roof has gone and some of the Adam frieze. The pictures had been removed to The National Library of Wales (Aberystwyth). The statue of Joshua Ward, a quack doctor who was buried in Westminster Abbey and who was called 'Spot' Ward from a birthmark, remains. It was the work of Agostino Carlini and was presented to the Society in 1792.

Temporarily leaving the Strand, by Waterloo Bridge on the south side, the walker comes to Waterloo Road. Here, on the east side, is ST. JOHN THE EVANGELIST CHURCH. It was built in 1823-4 and was one of four churches erected to commemorate the Peace that followed Waterloo. The others were: St. Matthew's, Brixton; St. Mark's, Kennington; and St. Luke's, Norwood. There was a fine stained glass window of the Crucifixion. On the night of 8th December 1940 a bomb ripped off the roof and demolished the interior. There were 150 people in the crypt below, but there were no casualties.

Returning over Waterloo Bridge to the Strand, the first 'island' church to be reached when walking eastwards is ST. MARY-LE-STRAND (1717). This has escaped the blitz. THE ROMAN BATH (in Strand Lane, at No. 162A) is not damaged, but the pipe which used to carry the water away was broken in the blitz.

17

SOMERSET HOUSE. This was built slowly between 1775 and 1790; the architect was Sir William Chambers. It took the place of the palace erected by Edward Seymour, Duke of Somerset and Protector to his nephew, Edward VI.

It was first used by the Royal Society, the Society of Antiquaries, and the Royal Academy. Later it became the 'nest of public offices' described by Trollope in *The Three Clerks.* Now it houses the Department of Inland Revenue, the office of the Registrar-General of Births, Deaths, and Marriages, and the Probate Registry.

The river front was bombed, but the damage was not of a very serious character. The finely decorated rooms, which were used by the societies mentioned above, are intact, as also is the somewhat unsightly group in the quadrangle representing George III attended by Father Thames. It was the work of John Bacon, R.A. (1780). In the basement of the present building are still five tombstones of some members of the Court who were buried in the old chapel in the latter part of the seventeenth century.

KING'S COLLEGE (south side, east of Somerset House). It was designed by Sir Robert Smirke and opened in 1834. It completed the river front of Somerset House, in accordance with the plans of Sir William Chambers for the latter building. The east end of the river front has been destroyed.

A little further on is

ST. CLEMENT DANES CHURCH. It dates from 1680, and is probably the third on the site. The plans were Wren's, and his work was commemorated by a tablet in the gallery. The superintending architect was Edward Pierce. Evelyn called it 'a pretty built and contrived church'. There was an ornate ceiling, adorned with the Royal Arms, and much good carving, particularly on the pulpit. This was ascribed, for no particular reason, to Grinling Gibbons. The church was attended by Samuel Johnson, and his pew, in the north gallery, was marked by a tablet in 1851. A memorial window, showing Johnson, Burke, Garrick, Goldsmith, Boswell, Mrs. Carter, and a dog, was installed in the north gallery in 1909, in commemoration of the bi-centenary of Johnson's birth. For some years the Johnson Society of London had held an annual memorial service here, sometimes placing a laurel wreath at the foot of Percy Fitzgerald's statue, erected outside, at the east end, in 1910.

It was the London church of Devonians and Australians, and of course the Danes. It is said that the first church on the site was a wooden one for ninth-century Danes who had married English wives. On the 14th April 1940 there was held, in view of the recent German invasion of Denmark, a special service in the Danish language.

In 1941 the crypt was explored for the first time for nearly a hundred years. To quote Mr. E. A. Young, a churchwarden and one-time bell-ringer, in *The*

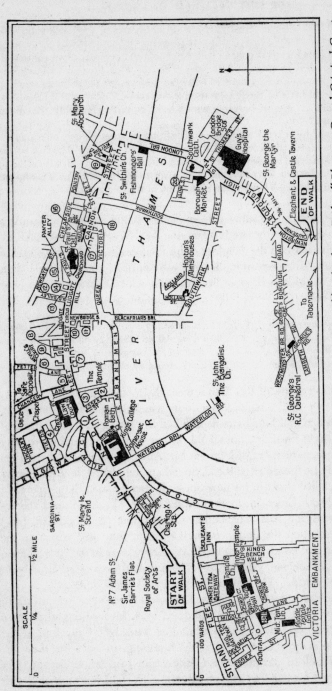

WALK I. STRAND TO THE ELEPHANT AND CASTLE. I. *St. Clement Danes Church.* 2. *Essex Gateway.* 3. *Twining's shop.* 4. *Royal College of Surgeons.* 5. *St. Dunstan's-in-the-West Church.* 6. *Moravian Chapel.* 7. *Serjeants' Inn.* 8. *Wine Office Court.* 9. *Dr. Johnson's House.* 10. *St. Bride's Church.* 11. *Bridewell Place.* 12. *Central Criminal Court.* 13. *St. Martin's Church.* 14. *Stationers' Hall.* 15. *Paternoster Row.* 16. *St. Augustine's Church.* 17. *Cordwainers' Hall.* 18. *St. Mildred's Church.* 19. *Salters' Hall.* 20. *Site of Bishop of Winchester's Palace.*

New Rambler (the organ of the Johnson Society of London) for January 1944:

The crypt, we found, extended under half the church and below the two vestries. It has been approached by steps on both sides. The roof is of groined vaulting, carried on brick piers and stone columns. It is very massive, yet the columns standing under the nave, in rows of three, seem to give the crypt an architectural value. The floor I could not see as it was covered with a layer of earth (probably containing human remains).

An Act was passed in 1851, prohibiting burials in urban areas. Shortly after this the overseers made a general clearance of the cells and their contents. The best of the coffins were re-enclosed in a newly formed chamber, and all else uniformly spread to a depth of 30 inches in a layer over the floor, always closely packed with earth, and covered with quicklime. Thus leaving all seemly, as we find it today.

Three times the church suffered from enemy action and it is now only a shell. A few weeks after the last 'incident' the Rev. W. Pennington Bickford, the rector, who married the daughter of his predecessor, died—it was said of a broken heart. After cremation his ashes were buried near the marble altar, where a few weeks later those of his wife were added. There is now a brass plaque in the ruin; it bears the following inscription:

Near this spot rest the remains of William Pennington Bickford, beloved rector of St. Clement Danes for 31 years, died June 12, 1941, from shock and grief caused by the destruction of this church by enemy action, also of Louie, his wife, who died September 5, 1941.
They were lovely and pleasant in their lives and in their death they were not divided.

With the destruction of the church went the Johnson pew and window. There also disappeared some wooden doors which came from Thrale Place, Streatham. When that house was demolished in 1863, several inhabitants of Streatham bought furniture, household fittings, house and garden property of various kinds, in memory of Johnson. Mr. Alfred Coleman, who was then building Holly Lodge, 29 High Road, Streatham, purchased three mahogany doors and installed them in his new house. It later became the property of his son, Dr. Frank Coleman. In 1931 Holly Lodge was demolished and replaced by shops and flats. The building contractors (B. Goodman, Ltd.) generously presented the doors to Dr. Coleman, who gave them to the Johnson Society of London. For a brief period they were in the vicar's house, The Anchorage, Clement's Inn Passage. From there they went to the church, where they perished. The pulpit is at St. Paul's Cathedral.

The tower stands, but the bells came down. There were ten of them, and in addition there was a sanctus bell dated 1578. Most of the others were dated 1693; two were recast about a hundred years ago. Only four of the bells were not cracked as a result of the bombing. In 1920 the Rev. W. Pennington Bickford instituted an Oranges and Lemons service on 31st March. This was for children and, on leaving, each child was presented with one of each of the fruits, whilst the bells played the old nursery rhyme. Farthings found amongst the ruins after the blitz were fancied by some journalists to have reference to the line of the rhyme which runs, 'I owe you five farthings'. The explanation was that they had been put in the collection bag and afterwards kept in a box, the contents of which became scattered.

ON PASSING ST. CLEMENT DANES

Clement Danes stands all forlorn
And destitute;
Bells that rang out yestermorn
To-day lie mute.

I hear children in my mind
All singing there;
But oranges are hard to find
And lemons rare.

Shall I ever hear again
The welcome chime
Ringing out from Clement Danes
The ancient rhyme?

Calling little folk to stand
In happy throng
Children singing in the Strand
A merry song.

HAROLD ADSHEAD

ESSEX STREET is on the south side of St. Clement Danes Church. At the south end is a damaged gateway, probably erected about 1662. It may have appertained to Essex House, demolished about 1680. Whilst the general opinion has been that it was its water-gate, there are those who think it was nothing but an ornamental terminal to the street when it was laid out by Dr. Nicholas Barbon—one of London's earliest speculative builders—on the site of the old house.

The Charles Lamb Society met in the Gatehouse Restaurant for a time in the winter of 1940-1, after being bombed out of another restaurant in the same street. The Gatehouse was then bombed, and they had to move again. The Society was inaugurated at Essex Hall in the early part of 1935. Essex Hall, originally the first chapel of the 'One God-ites' as Lamb called them (his Aunt Hetty sometimes attended—see *My Relations*) was built in 1778. It has been entirely destroyed. It stood at the Strand end of Essex Street on the west side and was the headquarters of British Unitarianism until a flying bomb came in July 1944. They were then removed to Gordon Square.

ROYAL COURTS OF JUSTICE (north side of the Strand). They were completed in 1882. The architect, G. E. Street, had then died. His successor was his son, who was assisted by (Sir) Arthur Blomfield.

There has been bombing on several occasions. The Court of Criminal Appeal and No. 3 Divorce Court were damaged. The Judges' Room was wrecked. A notice was once placed on the gateway: 'No thoroughfare to Carey Street' (Bankruptcy Court.)

On the south side of the Strand, just east of St. Clement Danes Church, is *TWINING'S SHOP*, the oldest firm of teamen in London. It was founded in 1706 and has been on the same site ever since.

In January 1941 the premises were severely damaged but, as a temporary expedient, it was found possible to fix up the front half of the shop, and so it has remained open throughout the war. Part of the old counter, the chairs, some of the old glass doors of the showcases, and a clock two hundred years old, were salvaged. The old ledgers, one containing the account of Sir Christopher Wren in 1718—his tea was from twenty to twenty-four shillings a pound and his coffee six shillings a pound—and other documents had been sent to a place of safety at the outbreak of war.

The premises will be rebuilt and it is hoped that well before 1956—when the firm will celebrate the 250th anniversary of its founding—they will be back again in full strength at the old place.

THE TEMPLE

By Devereux Court (west of Twinings) the reader can enter the Temple. *FOUNTAIN COURT* is first approached. The fountain is associated with Lamb and Dickens. The former said of its water (*Old Benchers of the Inner Temple,* 1821): 'which I have made to rise and fall, how many times! to the astoundment of the young urchins, my contemporaries, who, not being able to guess at its recondite machinery, were almost tempted to hail the wondrous work as magic.' Dickens (*Martin Chuzzlewit* 1843-4) introduced it as a courting place of John Westlock and Ruth Pinch. The fountain was bricked up for the utilitarian purpose of an A.F.S. tank early in 1940, but is now revealed much as Dickens and Lamb saw it.

The building immediately south of it is the
MIDDLE TEMPLE LIBRARY. There were here approximately 70,000 books when it was first severely blasted (December 1940). About 50,000 of these were blown off their shelves and about 8,000 were damaged. The only one beyond repair was *Decisions of the Court of Southern Rhodesia* (1915), but this has been replaced by another copy presented by the 'reporter' of that volume, now a Supreme Court Judge in South Africa.

East of the Fountain is the
MIDDLE TEMPLE HALL, erected between 1562 and 1570. Repairs were carried out in 1699 and 1745; in 1757 the exterior was 'improved' by a casing

of stone and its original red-brick character destroyed. The entrance tower dates from 1832. The Hall is 100 ft. long and 40 ft. wide. The hammer-beam roof is the best of the period in England. There is a richly carved minstrels' gallery with two fine doors beneath. The long table was presented by Queen Elizabeth and is said to have been made of oak from Windsor Forest. There is a serving table (a 'cupboard') the wood of which is said to have come from Drake's ship the *Golden Hind*.

The Hall has been hit five times but the damage can be made good. A temporary corrugated iron roof was erected after the last attack in 1944. Permanent restoration is now in progress. The stained glass windows had been removed. Neither the long table nor the 'cupboard' has sustained serious damage.

Beyond the Hall is Middle Temple Lane. To the left is all that remains of *BRICK COURT*. Goldsmith's Chambers (here he died in 1774) were badly hit. The small part that remained has been demolished. The tablet on the façade, designed by Percy Fitzgerald, was destroyed. Later residents were the poet Praed (c. 1830), and Thackeray (1853-9).

South of Brick Court, on the east side of Middle Temple Lane, is *CROWN OFFICE ROW*. No. 2, where Lamb was born, was badly damaged and what remained was demolished. The memorial tablet was broken but not destroyed. It was inscribed with another quotation from the essay *Old Benchers of the Inner Temple*: 'Cheerful Crown Office Row (place of my kindly engendure) . . . a man would give something to have been born in such places.'

Immediately south of Crown Office Row are *TEMPLE GARDENS* where is a Lamb memorial. It was placed there in 1930 and consists of the figure of a boy holding in his hand a book upon which is inscribed a passage from the essay last quoted: 'Lawyers were children once.' It was removed for safety. The Gardens have been little affected and the fine wrought-iron gate remains. It dates from 1730. Whilst the winged horse of the Inner Temple still surmounts it, the arms of Gray's Inn have gone. In the Gardens there is still the kneeling black figure supporting a sundial. It dates from about 1700 and is said to have come from Italy. It was brought here from Clement's Inn about 1905. There are five other sundials in the Temple: one at the back of Essex Court; two in Brick Court; one in Pump Court; and one in Middle Temple Gardens. The only one that was destroyed was in Middle Temple Lane.

PUMP COURT, which runs east out of Middle Temple Lane, has also suffered much, but the north side is intact. Here at No. 6, on the second floor, is a tablet commemorating the chambers of Alfred Harmsworth, father of Viscounts Northcliffe and Rothermere. There is a legal scholarship in his honour.

Pump Court leads to the

TEMPLE CHURCH. The round church was consecrated by Heraclius, Patriarch of Jerusalem, in 1185. The chancel dates from 1240. There was much restoration under Wren in 1681-3. In 1828 the beautiful arcading was restored by Sir Robert Smirke, the architect of the Inner Temple. A few of the forty sculptured heads date from this period but some are very much older. In 1840 the pavement was lowered about sixteen inches and numerous inscribed gravestones were removed to the north churchyard, where they can still be seen. There was almost a complete rebuilding of the 'Round' and hardly any of the external wall is ancient.

The western door is a very interesting feature. It probably dates from 1185, though there has been some restoration of the jambs. The half-length statues are supposed to represent, on the north, Henry II with three Templars, to whom he is presenting the charter of the foundation, and on the south, the Patriarch Heraclius, with three attendant clergy. There is an intermixture of foliage, tooth moulding and lozenges—the last perhaps due to Saracenic influence. The porch was probably built about ten years later, and connected with a cloister. The present one is modern. The cloisters were rebuilt by Wren in 1681 after a fire two years before. As in the case of Windsor Town Hall the pillars were formal—they did not support the building above. The present writer once saw a painter's brush inserted between the top of one and the lower part of the building above. The cloisters have gone.

The 'Round' was most famous for the nine effigies of knights, probably not Templars, as was once supposed. They were restored in 1840.

There was a beautiful font which was a copy of one from Alphington, near Exeter. The ornamentation was interlaced arcading, above which was a row of scenes from the chase.

The church suffered badly in the blitz. The fine Purbeck marble pillars remain, though they have been weakened and some part of the building's weight is now borne by heavy steel girders with concrete bases. All the monuments and decorative work have vanished, except the heads already mentioned. These are intact. Lamb refers to them—remarkable to relate, his only reference to the Temple Church—in his Elian essay *My First Play* (1821) as 'grotesque Gothic heads (seeming to me then replete with devout meaning) that gape, and grin, in stone around the inside of the old Round Church (my church) of the Templars'.

The conical roof, which has gone, dated only from 1840. With one exception the effigies have been destroyed. The survival is that of Lord de Ros (d. 1227). He was one of the twenty-five barons elected to compel King John to observe Magna Carta, and was excommunicated by Pope Innocent III for resisting the king when the former had absolved him from his oath. The effigy had been boarded up. Some monuments have been destroyed.

The following are the most important. A Purbeck marble effigy of Sylvester de Everden, Bishop of Carlisle, representing him attired in mass vestments, mitre, and gloves, with his right hand raised in benediction. He died in 1255. A monument to Edmund Plowden, Treasurer of the Middle Temple during the erection of the Hall. It was an altar tomb with a canopy, beneath which was a painted effigy of Plowden with his head on a cushion and his hands in prayer. He was wearing a skull cap and a long cloak. There was a fine marble bust of Richard Hooker, who died in 1600. It was standing on two volumes representing the famous *Laws of Ecclesiastical Polity*. The bust was the work of Alfred Gatley (1851). Richard Martin, Recorder of London, who died in 1615 had a monument showing him wearing a flowing scarlet robe, and kneeling on an embroidered and tasselled cushion before a small prayer-desk, with an open book in his left hand. There was a tablet in memory of John Selden, of *Table Talk* fame. He died in 1654. There was also a tablet to James Howell, who died in 1666. He left a wish to be buried 'in the long walke neare the doore which goes up the steeple'. He is famous to-day for his Familiar Letters (*Epistolae Ho-elianae*). They were published in four volumes (three written in the Fleet Prison) between 1645 and 1655. Another tablet was in memory of Edward Thurlow, Lord Chancellor and friend of William Cowper. He died in 1806.

In the triforium was a tablet in honour of Oliver Goldsmith. The stone on the north side of the church inscribed 'Here lies Oliver Goldsmith' does not mark his grave. It was placed there in 1860, eighty-six years after his death. There is every reason to believe that its position is approximately correct. The two bewigged figures on large monuments to the east of it commemorate John Hiccock who died in 1726 and Samuel Mead who died in 1733. They attract attention beyond their merits, and one was once represented in a book on London as Oliver Goldsmith. The stone coffins in the lower part of the graveyard are probably of thirteenth-century date.

Opposite the porch is

HARE COURT. It has not changed at all. It is still 'the gloomy churchyard-like court' that it was to Lamb when he lived in Inner Temple Lane (1808-17).

On the east side of the church was the Master's House, erected in 1670 and altered and restored in 1764. It has entirely disappeared.

South of the church was

LAMB BUILDING. Here lived Thomas Day, the eccentric author of *Sandford and Merton*, and (Sir) William Jones between 1765 and 1776. It also was the residence of Thackeray's Pendennis. Except for a short flight of stone steps which led to the door, it has been destroyed.

INNER TEMPLE HALL (south-east of the church) was erected in 1870, on the site of a much earlier one. It had some relics of that building, such as stone brackets of about 1500, two Elizabethan doors elaborately carved on one side, and a wall painting, the work of Sir James Thornhill in 1709, showing Pegasus leaping from the summit of Mount Helicon. There were two effigies of Knights Templars and two of Knights Hospitallers. The Hall has been reduced to a shell.

INNER TEMPLE LIBRARY stood at the east end of Crown Office Row. There is now nothing left. The little that remained after bombing had to be pulled down. The Library, in 1939, contained about 90,000 volumes, legal and general. After the severe damage in May 1941 about 45,000 books were sent out of London, so that the same number, mainly legal, was lost. Amongst these were a fine collection of reports of trials, a very extensive collection of Parliamentary papers (commencing from the early nineteenth century), the files of the *London Gazette* (from the seventeenth century, when it was entitled the *Oxford Gazette*, down to the present day), Journals of the House of Lords and of the House of Commons, a large number of maps (mainly early maps of London) and many early law books.

Charles Lamb wrote (*Old Benchers of the Inner Temple*): 'They have lately gothicized the entrance to the Inner Temple-hall, and the library front, to assimilate them, I suppose, to the body of the hall, which they do not at all resemble. What is become of the winged horse that stood over the former? a stately arms!' The winged horse was discovered about ten years ago and installed on the Library staircase. It has sustained some damage.

The old chambers at 4 and 5 King's Bench Walk, for some unknown reason ascribed to Wren, are intact. They date from 1678 and 1684.

INNER TEMPLE GATEWAY and 'Prince Henry's Room' over it (1610), the MIDDLE TEMPLE GATEWAY constructed by Wren (1684), and the WHITEFRIARS GATEWAY (1676) are all undamaged.

In 1916 a colony of rooks established themselves in The Temple (in the elm tree in Fountain Court). It was thought they might have been immigrants from the old rookery in Gray's Inn which had been deserted the previous year.

Frightened by the alarums and excursions of the Second World War, a pheasant appeared in The Temple in October 1940 during the blitz. It was chased into oblivion by a Temple cat.

LINCOLN'S INN

It can be approached from the Strand by way of Sardinia Street, on the east side of Kingsway.

The Old Hall (so called because it was built in 1489–91, though it was practically rebuilt in 1926-8), the New Hall, built from designs of Philip Hardwick in 1845, and the Chapel (1623, with an extension at the west end, 1883) have suffered little damage, and this mainly to modern glass. The only ancient glass in the Chapel was removed for safety. The windows in the New Hall had some good heraldic glass which has gone. The windows in the Old Hall and Library were not of much value. No books were lost.

Many chambers were damaged but none beyond repair. The east gate to Chancery Lane (1518) is practically undamaged.

CHANCERY LANE has been damaged at the north end. There was the famous Safe Deposit, now entirely gone. Here had been preserved the original drawings for Banister Fletcher's *History of Architecture,* probably the most successful book ever published by Batsford. Three months after the fire they were recovered. They were in a sodden state and odorous, but were carefully repaired by Ernest Zaehnsdorf, the well-known binder of Shaftesbury Avenue.

ROYAL COLLEGE OF SURGEONS (Lincoln's Inn Fields, south side). It was erected 1835-7 from the designs of Sir Charles Barry, and housed a museum, a theatre, and a library. It has been badly damaged by bombs. The following exhibits have been lost: the plaster cast of the hand of Patrick Cotter, the Irish giant; the skeleton of the elephant 'Chunee'—for long the principal exhibit at Exeter Change in the Strand; the iron pivot of a trysail driven through the body of John Taylor at London Docks (1831); and the mummy of the wife of Dr. Van Butchell. On her death in 1775 it was made to the order of the bereaved husband who afterwards married again. He then found it convenient to assign the deceased lady to the Royal College of Surgeons. They provided her with lodging but no clothes although, until banishment from her former home, the corpse had been elegantly attired. In 1941 the lady, thus unburied for 166 years, disappeared through enemy action. She was perhaps cremated. The skeletons of Charles Byrne (he was 7 ft. 8½ in. when he died in 1783) and of Jonathan Wild, the notorious criminal who was executed in 1725, were sent into the country and thus saved.

The site to the east, formerly occupied by the College of Estate Management, has now been acquired by the Royal College of Surgeons. Sir William Collins has given a second donation of £100,000 for the rebuilding and extension, provided that any part of the site not required by the Surgeons is offered to the Royal College of Physicians (now in Pall Mall East). In the ruins of the College of Estate Management, men of the National Fire Service set up a piggery. A number of piggeries were to be seen in London during the War, the first being at Clapham Police Station, Union Grove. When Mr. R. S. Hudson, Minister of Agriculture, made a tour of inspection he found twenty-nine pigs there.

In Portsmouth Street, south-west of Lincoln's Inn Fields, is the old shop which once bore the inscription:

The Old Curiosity Shop
Immortalised by Charles Dickens.

The late Mr. W. T. Cotter, for many years a highly respected churchwarden of the parish of St. Clement Danes, once had an office opposite. He told the present writer that he heard a guide say, 'This is the Old Curiosity Shop, immoralized by Charles Dickens.' The shop front has become more moral now. The lying inscription has been blitzed away. No one with any knowledge of Dickens accepted it. Amongst several reasons for rejection was the fact that it was not an old curiosity shop when Dickens wrote his novel (1840).

FLEET STREET

Walking south out of Chancery Lane one reaches Fleet Street. It is remarkable that, despite the blitz, there is hardly any break in the frontage of 'the Street of Ink'. There was trouble enough in the vicinity, but the main thoroughfare for the most part escaped. The difficulties of the pressmen have been most interestingly set out in *Fleet Street Blitzkrieg Diary* by Gordon Robbins (Chairman of Benn Bros., Ltd. and former President of the Institute of Journalists). The following relates to the last heavy raid on the City on 10th May 1941:

It cannot be denied that London is beginning to look very grimy. The demolition work that is going on on damaged buildings sends clouds of dust whirling about the streets to add to the masses of paper blown hither and thither from damaged offices. . . .

There were many minor inconveniences, such as the cutting off of the gas supply. On Monday, too, the milk delivery for the canteen failed for the first time. The post has remained exceptionally good, but the telephone service has been extremely difficult. It was impossible on Monday or Tuesday to make any outward calls, although any incoming ones could be received.

Communications continued to be very difficult all through Tuesday. In fact, from the point of view of getting about the City, this was clearly the worst raid up to date. There was a police cordon for wheeled traffic shutting off virtually the whole area between Blackfriars Bridge and Ludgate Circus, and London Bridge and Bishopsgate. Queen Victoria Street, Ludgate Hill, Cheapside, Cannon Street and the Bank circus were all barred, and even for pedestrians some astonishingly circuitous routes had to be taken.

Coming from London Bridge to Fleet Street for example, the only way for a walker on a morning on which the whole City seemed to be on the tramp, was to proceed by King William Street, the Bank, Old Jewry, Gresham Street, Milk Street, Cheapside, St. Paul's Churchyard, Godliman Street, Queen Victoria Street, New Bridge Street, and Ludgate Circus—a weirdly serpentine course with half-way up Queen Victoria Street, a narrow path between piles of debris. Fleet Street remained without buses, although it had a certain amount of wheeled traffic. The pavements were dangerous, as every man-hole cover remained where it had blown off. Bouverie Street and the upper part of Fetter Lane were still closed and the roadway in each case was in a shocking mess. . . .

Even by Friday the newspaper district was looking far from normal. Ludgate Hill was still blocked by masses of wreckage from the blowing-up of unsafe buildings at the lower end, and smoke was still coming from the ruins of Serjeants' Inn. Fleet Street was somewhat safer for pedestrians, as most of the man-hole covers had been got back into position. There were still, however, no buses running and communication with Outer London remained far from easy. The interruption of the District Railway service on the vital link between the Mansion House and Victoria was seriously felt, as was the chaotic running of the South London trams, although some had begun coming over Blackfriars Bridge. For the City, it has been a walking week.

ST. DUNSTAN'S-IN-THE-WEST CHURCH. There was a church here, at the latest, in the latter part of the twelfth century. This medieval building escaped the Great Fire. It was rebuilt, from the designs of John Shaw, in 1831-3. Many monuments remained from the old church. The best known was in memory of Hobson Judkin, 'The Honest Solicitor', who died in 1812.

Early in 1944 a bomb pierced the roof, but happily did little damage to the interior, and a wedding arranged for the next day was duly celebrated. None of the monuments was damaged, nor the stained glass window in memory of Izaak Walton (1895). The statue of Queen Elizabeth (from old Ludgate, 1586) over the entrance to the adjoining school was screened by a mass of brick, as also was the bust of Lord Northcliffe. Undamaged, too, was the old clock (1671) which was taken to the Marquis of Hertford's villa about 1830, to be returned to the church by Viscount Rothermere in 1935. The two figures, in Cowper's words, beat 'alternately in measured time'. In the porch of the schoolroom King Lud and his two sons (also from Ludgate) show that they have stood up to the blitz. One of the sons was said to have been a pro-Roman Quisling when just two thousand years ago this year (1946) Caesar invaded these islands!

East of St. Dunstan's Church is Fetter Lane. Here was the *MORAVIAN CHAPEL.* It was on the south side of Nevill's Court. The building was of uncertain date; some writers ascribed it to the early seventeenth century, others to the time of Charles II. It had associations with Dr. Goodwin, founder of the Independent church of which the City Temple was the offshoot, and also with Richard Baxter and the Wesley brothers. It had no architectural beauty to commend it, but was precious in its memories to 'chappellers', as one of Thomas Hardy's characters would have said. It was so thoroughly bombed that it has left not a wrack behind.

North of the Moravian Chapel is *NEVILL'S COURT.* The last old house here (No. 10) has been destroyed. It is believed to have been erected about 1662 and was a fine example of the type of residence of a City merchant in the Stuart period. It had a porch, and a wide front door, heavily protected on the inner side. The window frames were fitted with glazing bars of thick section, and the upper sashes were immovable; the lower sashes slid on rollers. The staircase was massively built; the newels were so high and the railings so wide that it was a difficult, sometimes an impossible, task to convey large furniture to the upper rooms. The closet cupboards were deep. The panelling, where remaining, was much overlaid with paint. The ceilings, when stripped of paper, disclosed dark-coloured beams of noble dimensions. The attic rooms were lighted by as many as twelve windows in the front alone. 'Antiquaries', said J. Paul de Castro (in a most interesting article in *Notes and Queries*, 28th June 1941) 'were struck by their similarity to the attic windows in the old silk-weavers' mansions in Spitalfields.' James Keir Hardie, M.P. lived in this house (it was on the south side and had a long front garden) for some years. He left it in 1915, to die in a nursing home near Glasgow the same year.

SERJEANTS' INN (south side). It was almost wiped out on the 16th May 1941. All the eighteenth-century houses (some designed by the Adam brothers) have gone. The 'gloomy house opposite the pump', which 'had the aspect of a strong box' wherein Thomas Coventry lived (see Lamb's essay *Old Benchers of the Inner Temple*), was amongst them. The pump also has disappeared. The house of Delane, editor of *The Times* 1841-77, is among those that have vanished.

Through Wine Office Court (at No. 145), Gough Square is reached. Here is

DR. JOHNSON'S HOUSE. It was built about 1700. Johnson resided here from 1748-59, the period of *The Rambler* and the *Dictionary*. Lord Harmsworth (in *The New Rambler* for January 1946) wrote as follows of the damage:

Its escape from destruction may be described as almost providential. Far beyond it in the direction of Holborn, and right into the heart of Gray's Inn, is to this day a scene of Pompeiian desolation. . . .

The trouble in Gough Square began on the night of the 29th December 1940 when blazing material from a neighbouring printers' ink factory set the roof alight. The next morning it was possible to walk on the floor of the Dictionary garret on the red tiles of Dr. Johnson's roof. The great crosswise beams supporting the roof were charred but sound. Altogether the house was affected by the Nazi blitz on five occasions. The second most serious attack was on the 18th July 1944. The result of this was the dislocation of panelling and of the characteristic partitions separating the rooms on the first floor. After the first attack the portable treasures of the house were salvaged with the assistance of firemen and by the courtesy of Lord Rothermere and his co-Directors of the *Daily Mail* were removed to Carmelite House, and none of them has suffered the slightest harm.

During the War years the house, while not inaccessible to the public, afforded much needed shelter to the men and women in the Auxiliary Fire Service in the neighbourhood. A Club was formed, comfortable furniture was bought or borrowed, and sometimes during the most dangerous periods the old place resounded (as Dr. Johnson would doubtless have wished) with laughter and fun.

The damaged knights' effigies in the Inner Temple Hall. They are three of the four bronze statues which were designed by H. H. Armstead, R.A., in
1875

St. Clement Danes, described by Evelyn as 'a pretty built and contrived church' decorated for the re-dedication of the bells in 1920. Dr. Johnson's pew was at the front of the north gallery

Above. *The funeral service for the Rev. W. Pennington Bickford, rector of St. Clement Danes, in the ruins of the church.* Below. *The fallen bells and works of the carillon*

Above. *The fresco by G. F. Watts which covers the north wall of Lincoln's Inn Hall. The Hall lost only a few windows, mostly modern. Below. Damage in the beautiful library of Lambeth Palace, which contained about 42,000 books and 1,300 volumes of MSS*

Lord Harmsworth paid tribute to the 'Devotion and courage exhibited by Mrs. Rowell, the Custodian, by her daughter Betty and her husband'. Mrs. Rowell's mother, the first Custodian, died shortly after the first 'incident'.

Through the bombing of the Dictionary garret there was revealed the existence of a ship's mast beneath the floor.

In 1945 Lord Harmsworth presented a piece of rafter from the garret to Captain Parker who had called at the house and asked for a souvenir for the Boswell Club of Chicago, with which his father was connected. It was welcomed as a 'real piece of old England', and converted into a gavel and stand.

The house can still be visited, but owing to delay in executing the necessary repairs only a few exhibits are there.

ST. BRIDE'S CHURCH (south side). This fine Wren church was completed in 1680. It retained its gallery (as did Christ Church, Newgate) and it could accommodate about 1,100 people. It measured 111 ft. by 57 ft. The ceilings of the aisles were groined; the pilasters finely set off the huge pillars. The east window represented Rubens's *Descent from the Cross*.

On the dreadful night of 29th December 1940 the church was reduced to a shell, but the spire (one of Wren's finest) survived. It is 226 feet high—the greatest altitude in the City apart from St. Paul's Cathedral. The following memorials have survived: tablet to Dr. James Mollins, physician to Charles II and James II (1686); gravestone of Samuel Richardson (1761); brass tablet erected on the north wall by the Stationers' Company in 1889 to commemorate the bi-centenary of the novelist's birth; tablet to Alderman Waithman, a Fleet Street draper who was five times Member of Parliament for the City (1833); brass plate in memory of Thomas Weelkes, given by the Madrigal Society to commemorate the tercentenary of his death (1923). The tablets commemorating Sir Arthur Pearson, Sir George Newnes, and Sir Edmund Robbins (Vice-President of the Newspaper Press Fund) have gone. Twelve bells fell from the tower and were broken.

The registers have survived, including the one containing the entry of the baptism of Samuel Pepys (2nd March 1633). The beautiful little font, which was probably used on this occasion (it was dated 1615) has been entirely destroyed; no trace of it was found. The plate has been preserved. This includes an inscribed cup and cover paten (1630), a bread dish (1671) and a mace (1703).

In the churchyard there is still the vault of the Holden family, dated 1657. Members of the family are mentioned in Pepys's Diary.

The fine gates, erected by the Newspaper Society in 1936 in memory of Valentine Knapp, its President from 1919-22, are untouched. The vicarage in Bridewell Place has survived.

LUDGATE HILL

There are large gaps on the north and south sides. On the north side the premises of Cassell and Co., Ltd. have entirely disappeared. This occurred in May 1941, through incendiary bombs and the inadequate supply of water. There, and in the warehouse at Watford, the firm lost about two million books. Outside their premises were carved in stone the heads of Shakespeare, Milton, and Wordsworth. A stone figure of 'La Belle Sauvage', the sign of the inn which was on the site, is intact and some day will be reinstated.

Other well-known shops on Ludgate Hill that disappeared at the same time were, on the south side, Treloar's carpet warehouse, a branch of Straker and Sons, Ltd., and the Sunday School Union. The sites are now concealed by a corrugated iron fence.

On the north side is the Old Bailey, where is the
CENTRAL CRIMINAL COURT. The present building was erected in 1902-7 from the designs of Edward W. Mountford. It has been twice hit— in 1940 and 1941. A high-explosive bomb shattered the Newgate Street end of the building and one of the Courts was put out of action.

The church of St. Martin (bearing on its façade a City Corporation tablet indicating the site of Ludgate) has survived undamaged.

A little farther east is the narrow Stationers' Hall Court. Here is
STATIONERS' HALL. It was completed in 1674, its predecessor having been burnt in the Great Fire. It was faced with Portland stone in 1800. There is some fine wainscoting, the work of Stephen College, an ultra-protestant joiner, who was executed at Oxford on a charge of treason in 1681. The screen is a fine piece of carving (late seventeenth century).

There are windows in the Hall commemorating Caxton presenting a specimen of his printing to Edward IV; William Tyndale; Thomas Cranmer; Shakespeare; St. Cecilia; and, again, Caxton.

The Hall was damaged by bombs, the roof being burnt. There was slight damage to the screen, which was then removed for safety. The stained glass windows have been damaged, but not seriously. The shields have survived. The banners have been damaged.

The court room has suffered most damage and, for the time, it cannot be used. The pictures of John Boydell (engraver) and Samuel Richardson (printer and novelist) have been injured; the picture of Mrs. Richardson has been destroyed.

The registers and plate are intact. The latter includes cups of 1674, 1676, and 1677; a tazza of 1684, and a pair of candlesticks of 1685.

On the 6th March 1946, for the first time since 1939, the Stationers revived an old custom. It derived from the will of John Norton, a City alderman who in 1612 left £150 to provide cakes and ale every Ash Wednesday to any liveryman of the Company who cared to come to Stationers' Hall and get them. The money was invested in City property which was lost in the blitz, so in 1946 the Company footed the bill. It was not large: for one thing the cakes were represented by small austerity buns.

ST. PAUL'S CATHEDRAL

It was designed by Sir Christopher Wren and erected between 1675 and 1710. It has emerged from the war scarred but, happily, not seriously damaged. It was well said by *The Times*, 'The Cathedral has become in these latter years more than ever a symbol of the unconquerable spirit that has sustained the fight. . . . None who saw will ever forget their emotions on the night when London was burning and the dome seemed to ride the sea of fire like a great ship lifting above smoke and flame the inviolable ensign of the golden cross.'

On the 12th September 1940 a heavy delayed-action bomb buried itself 27 ft. in the ground near the clock tower (immediately south of the granite posts). It was disposed of three days later by being conveyed to Hackney Marshes on a lorry under the command of Lieut. Davies, a Canadian. It was a magnificent achievement: an accident would have meant death to the whole squad. The crater the bomb made was 100 feet wide.

On the morning of 10th October, a bomb went through the outer roof of the Choir. A mass of debris fell and destroyed the high altar, which was quite modern (1888). Happily the Grinling Gibbons stalls were unimpaired though the Lord Mayor's stall was damaged.

On 29th December, the Cathedral had a remarkable escape. The Special Correspondent of *The Times* wrote:

At one time fires were raging all round the great Church, but it escaped almost without harm. Yesterday morning its doors were open, and in the Chapel of St. Dunstan a clergyman led a small congregation in prayer while outside the narrow streets were filled with pungent smoke, there was a continuous clatter as broken glass was shovelled up, interlaced hoses covered the roadways, the fire engines went on pumping, and here and there buildings still smouldered sombrely. Approaching from the west one had noticed shining out through the smoke that filled Ludgate Hill the fairy lights on the great Christmas tree on the steps of the Cathedral. Inside was another lighted tree, with around it gifts for evacuated children and men of the minesweepers.

It is proposed to erect a commemorative tablet in the Chapel of St. Michael and St. George.

On the 16th April 1941, a bomb fell on the north transept, pierced the saucer dome and exploded inside the Cathedral. The debris broke through the floor into the crypt. Almost all the stained glass (including windows given by the Goldsmiths', Drapers', and Musicians' Companies) was destroyed by blast and the iron framework was twisted and bent. Some monuments were damaged and the portico inside the north door, once part of the organ screen, was destroyed. On this was repeated the famous epitaph to Wren over his grave in the crypt: *Lector, si monumentum requiris, circumspice* (Reader, if you seek his monument, look around you).

On the same night there was found, a few feet from the eastern wall, a land mine 8 ft. high. A squad removed it in the course of four hours.

The monuments of St. Paul's Cathedral are all modern, with one exception. This is the one in memory of John Donne, Dean of St. Paul's, poet and prose writer, who died in 1631. It survived the Great Fire and stood in the south choir aisle. It shows the Dean standing in a shroud on a funeral urn in accordance with the painting made a few weeks before his death, mentioned by his friend and biographer, Izaak Walton. It was removed for safety.

There is to be a War Memorial Chapel in the eastern apse of the Cathedral to commemorate particularly the men of the fighting services who have died and been buried in Great Britain during the War, or have fallen in operations based on the British Isles. An appeal for funds has been launched by the American and British Commonwealth Association.

Sophie v. la Roche, a German visitor to London in 1786, wrote of St. Paul's Cathedral as follows: 'At first sight one cannot help wishing that Parliament would purchase a number of the surrounding houses and have them broken up so that the splendid pile might appear in all its dignity. For although a square has been railed off all round, yet both it and the neighbouring streets are still too narrow.' The breaking up has been done by her countrymen.

In the vacant spaces thus provided there has sprung up a profusion of flowers. These are shown in one of the illustrations to this book, and are welcomed in a poem by J. H. McNulty, which first appeared in the *City Press*.

LONDON PRIDE

Through centuries the ancient town
  Gave heart and soul to work and trade,
  Her ramparts strong her fortune made,
She cared not for the tyrant's frown.

Then death descended from the skies,
  And night and day she bore the blast,
  Stunn'd, scarr'd and battered, found at last
The terror cease, and new hope rise.

Then nature strove with tender care,
  With lavish and with loving hand,
  To heal the wounded, broken land,
And scatter'd flowers everywhere.

Where all was dead, new life appears,
Where all was dark, light shines again,
And beauty now replaces pain
The city bore through five dark years.

Not since the days of Roman might,
Not since the Norman here held sway,
Nor since her earliest, half-glimpsed day,
Has London seen so strange a sight.

Blooms purple, mauve and crimson glow
And gold, no mint has ever seen,
Bracken and grasses grow between
'Tis nature's City Flower Show.

Canon Alexander, in a paper on *The Survival of St. Paul's,* read at the Grocers' Hall on the 19th September 1945, said of the restoration fund for the Cathedral:

The first appeal was issued in the spring of 1914, a memorable year, and a few weeks later the criminal attack of Germany on Europe broke out. In the interval, finding that several members of our Royal house were contributing, I thought that possibly the German Emperor who, I understood, was deeply interested in St. Paul's, would like to join them, and I sent a letter to the then German Ambassador who replied, after a long delay, that His Imperial Majesty regretted his inability to subscribe. Hardly a month later the War unexpectedly burst upon us. I never was less sorry for the loss of any contribution.

The Chapter-house on the north side (the ground floor had been occupied by the City Livery Club) was gutted on the 29th December 1940. It was erected about 1712 and had some fine wrought iron balusters.

North of the Cathedral is

PATERNOSTER ROW

Its name has a religious derivation, but this is matter only for the antiquary. To most people it suggested not the fatherhood of God but the parentage of books. In early years, those of us who are older, knew that from 'the Row', as it was called for short, came most of our Sunday School prizes—from S. W. Partridge and Co., and the Religious Tract Society. To boys it was treasure trove in the matter of the latter publishing house, as from there came *The Boy's Own Paper*, which has never had its peer amongst boys' periodicals. Here, when we walked, we thought of books burgeoning to birth, and one rhymester, recalling perhaps Lamb's essay *Grace Before Meat*, asked why men should have Harvest Festivals

For rain that made potatoes grow
And be thankless for the books that fruitful authors drop,
For a publisher's good season up in Paternoster Row.

It had, too, its appeal for hunters of second-hand books, though this was less than that of Holywell Street and Charing Cross Road. Old Humphreys, 'bearded like the pard' and with a somewhat dilapidated person, savouring of Dickens's Solomon Krook, stood guard over a dirty, disorderly shop which, however, according to him, contained all things essential to eternal salvation in the matter of literature, though the reader might buy the pearl of great price by much boredom in its perusal. Later came Kiek's, a more spacious and salubrious shop.

The Row stood mainly, however, for publishers, as the Temple for lawyers and Harley Street for doctors and surgeons. The following firms were there when the War came:

Nicholson and Watson; John Hogg; A. Lewis, Ltd.; John Davis; Pickering and Inglis, Ltd.; Samuel Bagster and Sons, Ltd.; Elliott Stock; Robert Scott; Pitman, Hart and Co.; Sheed and Ward, Ltd.; Rider and Co.; J. F. Shaw and Co., Ltd.; Denis Archer; Hurst and Blackett, Ltd.; Hutchinsons and Co., Ltd.; John Long, Ltd.; Jarrolds, Ltd.; Leisure Library Co.; Andrew Melrose, Ltd.; Stanley Paul and Co., Ltd.; Selwyn and Blount, Ltd.; Skeffington and Son, Ltd.; T. C. and E. C. Jack, Ltd.; Thomas Nelson and Sons, Ltd.; William Blackwood and Sons, Ltd.; Longmans, Green and Co., Ltd.; Tablet Publishing Co., Ltd.

It had, too, its annals in the history of literature. Here, in 1719, was published *Robinson Crusoe*, and on the same site Longmans Green had been for over two hundred years when they were bombed out. Here had come Chatterton, who boasted in a letter to his sister that he was known at the Chapter House Tavern. In the same hostelry Johnson treated with the book-sellers in respect of the *Lives of the Poets*. To 'the Row', seventy years later, came Charlotte and Emily Brontë, *en route* to Brussels. Here, too, was a bust of Aldus Manutius, the Venetian printer who is mentioned in More's *Utopia* and who was the inventor of Italic type. It was erected by Samuel Bagster in 1820.

On the night of the 29th December 1940, the bombs rained down here and Paternoster Row was more completely destroyed than any other City thoroughfare of importance. All that remained were a few buildings at the east end. The devastation in respect of books has been indicated by Evan Pughe, the Deputy Chairman of Simpkin Marshall and Co. (1941) Ltd.:

On the night of 29th December 1940, Simpkin Marshall, Ltd., the greatest distributors of English books in the world, carrying the largest comprehensive stock, lost approximately four million books when their premises in Ave Maria Lane, Stationers' Hall Court, Stationers' Hall, Amen Corner, Paternoster Row, and Ludgate Hill, were entirely destroyed by the incendiary bombs of the enemy.

his disastrous fire eliminated everything. All the old records of the business going
ack a hundred and thirty years were destroyed; and, most important of all, the great
ataloguing system, the only one of its kind in the world, dating back for a hundred
nd fifty years. These catalogues were hand-written records of books, cross-referenced,
o that books on all subjects could be easily traced. These records could immediately
ive books that had been published on any subject during the hundred and fifty years
overed by them, the publisher, the date of publication, the price, the size of the book,
tc. They were invaluable and their loss will be felt by the reading public for many
ears to come.

The fitting comment was made by 'Sagittarius' in the *New Statesman*:

> Red roared the fire through the heart of London's City,
> Hurled from the clouds by a brute and savage foe,
> They who their own land robbed of light and learning
> Kindled the books here, a brand for London's burning,
> Lighted the bonfire of Paternoster Row.

Old-world Amen Court, west of Paternoster Row, is happily quite undamaged.

At the east end of Paternoster Row is
PANYER ALLEY. Here was the tablet showing a boy sitting on a bread
basket, underneath which was the inscription:

> When ye have sought the City round
> Yet still this is the highest ground.
> *August the 27th* 1688.

The boy was removed for safety to the vaults of the Central Criminal Court
and cannot be reinstated until there is some rebuilding of his old quarter.
The inscription is not quite accurate. Panyer Alley is 58 ft. above sea level;
Cornhill 60 ft.)

On the east side of the Cathedral are the ruins of
ST. AUGUSTINE'S CHURCH (Watling Street). There has been a
church on the site since the early part of the twelfth century. There were
repairs in the latter part of the sixteenth century and the church was burnt
in the Great Fire.

It was rebuilt by Wren (1683). The steeple was not completed until 1695.
It provided a good foil to the dome of St. Paul's Cathedral. The church
(51 ft. by 45 ft.) was divided into a nave and side aisles by six Ionic columns,
which were on remarkably lofty bases. The altar-piece had Corinthian
columns. The pulpit was of carved oak. It was modernized by (Sir) Arthur
Blomfield in 1878. There were no monuments of importance.

As a result of the blitz the church has been partly destroyed and has lost its
lead-covered spire, but the tower remains.

CANNON STREET

CORDWAINERS' HALL (north side, near St. Paul's Cathedral). The last Hall, the sixth on the site, was erected in 1909-10 from the designs of Howard Chatfield Clarke, F.R.I.B.A. It was 'of grey Portland stone, with a front elevation treated in the English phase of the Renaissance, with very little ornamentation. The front is dealt with in two heights, the lower being rusticated and containing two floors, the ground and mezzanine, and in the upper portion, which contains the court rooms and hall, an Ionic order is used, running throughout the two floors, and terminating with an open balustrade. The entrance doorway is executed in grey polished Aberdeen granite.' (*A Descriptive and Historical Account of the Guild of Cordwainers of the City of London*, by C. H. W. Mander, M.A., LL.M., Clerk of the Company, 1931.) The ground floor was occupied by a branch of the Westminster Bank.

A few relics of the former Hall (1788) remained. These were the chimney-pieces in the court room and reception room; a window erected to the memory of John Came (he was a benefactor to the Company and warden in 1765); his memorial urn; two escutcheons on wood from the Hall rebuilt after the Great Fire; and a set of pewter plates (c. 1700) unearthed from the cellars.

Joseph Chamberlain, father of the one-time Colonial Secretary, was a Master of the Company. The Hall contained two portraits of the latter. One represented him addressing a meeting (this was the unfinished work of C. W. Furse, A.R.A.); in the other (by Isaac M. Cohen) he was wearing the robes of the Garter. There were also portraits of Sir. J. Austen Chamberlain and Viscount Wakefield of Hythe.

The Company has some valuable plate. Most notable are: a porringer with 1666 hall-mark; a flat-lidded tankard (1679); a two-handled porringer (1684); six silver spoons with the Company's crest (presented 1719); a soup tureen and cover with the Company's arms (presented 1764); a silver gilt vase in memory of Joseph and Richard Chamberlain, former Masters (presented, in 1896), by the Rt. Hon. Joseph Chamberlain, M.P.; a silver gilt rose-water dish and ewer (presented in 1915, in memory of the Rt. Hon. Joseph Chamberlain, by his son, the Rt. Hon. Austen Chamberlain, and his grandson, Joseph Chamberlain); a silver model of the Nelson Monument in Trafalgar Square (1925); a silver model of the Company's previous Hall (1929).

The Company once possessed a literary treasure—a copy of *General Historie of Virginia, New England and the Summer Islands* by Captain John Smith. This first edition (1624) was given to the Company by the author, who wrote a letter of presentation on the blank back of the title page. It is not known whether Smith, one of the founders of Virginia (he was buried in the Church of St. Sepulchre, Newgate, where a brass tablet bears a eulogistic epitaph) was under any obligation to the Company. The book was presented by them to the Huntingdon Library in California.

The Hall has been destroyed except for the stone doorway. The chimney-pieces and the wooden escutcheons were lost. The Came window, the por-traits, and the plate were stored away and saved.

ST. MILDRED'S CHURCH, Bread Street (south side). There was a church here in the first half of the thirteenth century. It is not certain if this had been rebuilt before the Great Fire. Wren's church was completed in 1683.

It was a handsome structure. It had almost all the original woodwork and was the one City church with pews practically unchanged since its erection. The altar-piece was divided by Corinthian columns and pilasters and in-cluded paintings of Moses and Aaron. The pulpit was unsurpassed by any in the City; it had a magnificent sounding-board. The walls were panelled, and the City Corporation pew had figures of the lion and unicorn and an elegant sword rest. The only subjects for criticism were unsuitable stained glass windows, and ugly electric light standards before the reredos.

On the south wall was a tablet commemorating Sir Thomas Crispe, son of Sir Nicholas Crispe who was buried at Hammersmith Parish Church in 1666; the epitaph made mention of his father's fidelity to Charles I and Charles II.

The parish registers, dating from 1559, include the entry of the marriage of Shelley and Mary Wollstonecraft on 30th December 1816. It was this asso-ciation that once took Thomas Hardy to the church.

On the outside wall, through the generosity of Viscount Wakefield, there was placed, in 1932, a huge memorial to Admiral Phillip, first Governor of New South Wales (1788-93). He was born in Bread Street Ward in 1738. A map of Australia was above the bust and at the sides were panels showing the discovery of the site of Sydney (1788) and supplies being left there.

The church was entirely destroyed. Once again the tower was left but it was eventually demolished. It had no architectural feature to commend it. The memorial to Admiral Phillip was damaged but has been restored. The registers and plate have survived.

ST. SWITHIN'S CHURCH (north side of Cannon Street). A church here is first mentioned in 1236. It was rebuilt about 1420. This church was burnt in the Great Fire and rebuilt by Wren (1678). It had a fine octagonal domed roof with plaster moulding. The lower portion of the walls was panelled. The reredos had four panels divided by fluted pillars of the Corin-thian order. There was a good sword-rest dating from 1740. The only note-worthy monument was to Michael Godfrey who was killed by a cannon ball at the siege of Namur in 1695. The church has been reduced to a shell.

Embedded in the south wall is London Stone. This is quite undamaged and the Latin and English inscriptions are untouched.

In St. Swithin's Lane on the west side of the church is
SALTERS' HALL. The Salters' Company has been on the site since 1641.
The third Hall (the first was in Bread Street) was destroyed in the Great Fire.
The fourth was demolished in 1821.

The present Hall was built in 1823-7. It is semi-classical in style, with a
portico of the Ionic order. Its interior was small (71 ft. by 40 ft.) and handsome. In May 1941 the interior of the Hall and the surrounding buildings
were destroyed by fire. The columns, the entrance, and the whole façade are
still standing, though badly charred. Most of the Company's portraits—two
reputed to be by Reynolds—had been sent into the country and so were
saved. The most important documents had also been sent away. These included the original charter of James I (1608), the original charter of James II,
and the Grant of Arms (1530). A loving cup of 1716 and two others of about
the same date had been sent to the U.S.A.

The wrought-iron gateway at the entrance to the courtyard was erected
in the year of Queen Victoria's Jubilee (1887). The animal displayed there
and represented in the Company's arms is an ounce—'a name originally
given to the common lynx. . . . From sixteenth century applied to various
other small or moderate-sized feline beasts, vaguely identified' (*Oxford
English Dictionary*). It has occasioned some controversy amongst historians
of the Livery Companies. Some maintain that it should be an otter. Amongst
these is William Herbert (*History of the Twelve Great Livery Companies*,
1836). He wrote: 'Otters are well known, when taught, to drive fish into the
net, and might not unlikely be used in ancient time as serviceable on that
account; and, in this light, they were properly allusive.' The motto of the
Company is *Sal Sapit Omnia* (salt flavours all things).

ST. MARY ABCHURCH (Abchurch Lane, north side). There was a
church here in 1198, which was rebuilt by Wren, after the Great Fire, in
1686. It is almost square, measuring 63 ft. by 60 ft. It is surmounted by a
cupola which Sir James Thornhill embellished with paintings, the subject
being the adoration of the Deity. The altar-piece is a fine one, enclosed by
four Corinthian columns, with entablature and pediment, and displays above
the centre a gilded figure of a pelican with outstretched wings. The carved
festoons of fruit and flowers are after Grinling Gibbons. The pulpit is of
carved oak and a handsome font cover is ornamented with figures of the four
evangelists. The reredos is the largest of any City church and, at its apex, is
the monogram of James II surrounded by cherubs.

The dome of the church has been damaged and consequently Sir James
Thornhill's pictures have suffered. They can, however, be restored.

LONDON BRIDGE

On the north-west corner of London Bridge is
FISHMONGERS' HALL. The Company has been on this site since about
1504. The present Hall was erected in 1831-3. It is the most conspicuous of all
the Companies' Halls, with its classical portico facing the approach to the
Bridge. It was the first to suffer in the recent War. The court dining-room,
court drawing-room, and vestibule were completely burnt out and valuable
furniture destroyed. The banqueting hall is, however, intact save for two
large stained glass windows. A funeral pall with embroidered figures of St.
Peter, dated about 1500, and the dagger with which Sir William Walworth
struck down Wat Tyler (1381) have been preserved.

It has for some years been used as a British Restaurant—perhaps a loss of
status in the view of some City fathers. Still, the craft justifies such use.

On the south side of London Bridge is
SOUTHWARK CATHEDRAL. It was the church of St. Mary Overie
until 1540; St. Saviour's until 1905; from that date, Southwark Cathedral.
The architecture is of different dates, from c. 1220 (Choir and Lady Chapel)
to 1897, when Sir Arthur Blomfield completed the rebuilding of the nave.

There was no direct hit but a high explosive bomb dropped in the adjacent
Borough Market. Six people were killed and part of the churchyard wall was
destroyed. In the Cathedral the damage was confined almost entirely to
stained glass. The only old glass in the Cathedral (Elizabethan) was to be
found in the Harvard window in the chapel of the same name (a commem-
moration of the fact that John Harvard was baptized in what was then St.
Saviour's Church in 1607). All the best-known windows were destroyed.
These were in memory of Chaucer, Shakespeare, Alleyn, Massinger, Beau-
mont, Fletcher, Bunyan, Sacheverell, Johnson, Goldsmith and Cruden. They
dated from 1896 to 1903. The Shakespeare monument (1912) beneath the
window, showing a recumbent effigy in alabaster, with London Bridge,
Winchester Palace, and the Globe Theatre in the background, is intact, as
are all the other monuments (Gower, Lancelot Andrewes, etc.) and the
wooden bosses from the fifteenth-century roof. Four windows in the north
transept entirely escaped; the big west window is slightly damaged. A window commemorating Dr. Wood, a local physician, was removed for safety
(the glass was designed by J. N. Comper), as was the old glass in the Harvard
Chapel.

SOUTHWARK

On the west side of the Cathedral is
CLINK STREET, SOUTHWARK. Here, in an archway, was some
rubble walling. It was a fragment of the Bishop of Winchester's Palace and

dated from about 1340. In the course of demolition, consequent upon bombing, it was removed.

GUY'S HOSPITAL (St. Thomas's Street, east side of Borough High Street, near Southwark Cathedral) was completed about 1724 but the façade dates from 1773. It was first hit in September 1940, when all the operating theatres were damaged. In December of the same year, serious damage was caused to a section of the surgical building. In April 1944 the eastern wing of the main building was destroyed by fire. This contained some beautiful eighteenth-century rooms, used by the governors. The court room had on the ceiling paintings attributed to Sir James Thornhill.

The chapel, where the founder was buried, is undamaged, as also is his statue there (by Bacon) and the one in the courtyard (by Scheemakers). The alcove from old London Bridge (1762) has also survived.

There is a new building scheme.

In King's Head Yard (at 43 Borough High Street) excavations have been carried out by American, Dutch, and British archaeological students. Roman remains were discovered—wattle walls and the foundations of small rooms surrounding a central courtyard. Samian and Belgic pottery, coins, and the skeletons of three dogs were also unearthed. One day, when the medieval level had been reached, the excavators noticed on returning from lunch that there had been some disturbance of the earth. There was then found, several feet down, an old shoe with a label bearing the words: 'This shoe was worn by King Alfred.'

In Holland Street, a turning off Southwark Street are

HOPTON'S ALMSHOUSES. They were erected about 1740 under the will of Charles Hopton. There has been damage to the centre block and the south wing.

The oldest house in the Borough, dating from about 1680, is in the same street and on the same side of the road. It is undamaged.

Some little distance south of the Cathedral is

ST. GEORGE THE MARTYR'S CHURCH (Borough High Street) the Parish Church of Southwark. It was built in 1734-6 on a site occupied by a previous church for six centuries. It has a square tower at the west with an octagonal upper storey containing a clock. The steeple is very conspicuous. The church is sometimes called 'Little Dorrit's Church' because it figured in Dickens's novel. In the part of the churchyard separate from the church are tablets commemorating the adjacent Marshalsea Prison. There was some damage from a bomb in the vicinity.

Some distance west of this church off St. George's Circus is

ST. GEORGE'S (R.C.) CATHEDRAL. It was built in 1840-8 and the architect was A. W. Pugin. It was a handsome Gothic building, the clustered columns and large Perpendicular windows giving it a most stately appearance. Lack of funds led to the construction of a poverty-stricken roof. It was badly damaged in February and March 1941, when the roof was destroyed, and on three occasions by flying bombs in June and July 1944. The beautiful altar-piece in the north chapel was unharmed. The Cathedral can be restored.

Southwark had the largest air-raid shelter of any London Borough. This was the old City and South London Railway tunnel. It was opened on the 24th June 1940. There were eight entrances. It was 70 ft. deep and held at least 10,000 people. The cost of adaptation was £50,000.

Borough High Street leads to Newington Causeway, at the south end of which is the well-known Elephant and Castle Tavern. On the opposite side of the road is all that remains of

THE METROPOLITAN TABERNACLE. The first was erected in 1859-61 to accommodate the huge crowd that had gathered to hear the Rev. C. H. Spurgeon preach in New Park Street Chapel, and in the Surrey Music Hall. It was destroyed by fire in 1898. A new building was erected by 1900. It was very similar to the previous one having, as before, an imposing Corinthian portico. There were two galleries and it accommodated about three thousand. Bombs have destroyed the second Tabernacle, even as fire did the first one. The portico remains. There must be almost complete rebuilding but as, on the new County of London rebuilding plan, a main road is to cross the site, it will not be in the same place, though as close as possible to it. A building will be erected capable of accommodating two thousand people.

Walk 2

Queen Victoria Street ★ Austin Friars ★ Cheapside ★
Aldersgate Street ★ Cripplegate

QUEEN VICTORIA STREET

ON the north side, at Blackfriars end is
'*THE TIMES' OFFICE*. In September 1940 a high-explosive bomb fell
outside the building and made a huge crater in Queen Victoria Street. Considerable damage was caused. The following is an extract from an article by
F. P. Bishop (*Times House Journal*, October 1940):

The Manager has arrived and taken charge, and presently dawn is breaking. That
brings a new set of problems. Today's paper is all right; now we must think of tomorrow's. First, in the growing light, we make a full tour of inspection. There are
books and papers scattered about in the road; we peer at them with torches. Letters
signed by this or that member of the staff, circulars, telephone directories, pages from
a book about the Spanish war; nothing that really matters, at least let's hope not!

But what about to-night's paper? How is the classified department going to extract
from the appalling mess the advertisements booked to occupy the front and back
pages? And where are we going to put all the day staff? The editorial, managerial,
advertisement, accounts departments have all disappeared, and the library. The main
telephone switchboard is out of action. So are the tape machines. And the rooms that
can be made available are without windows and even without desks and chairs.

The mechanical superintendent, the architect, the electrician, were soon
on the job and business was carried on as usual. The subscription department
had to evacuate their rooms, but made such progress in this that by 4 o'clock
they had prepared the postal wrappers for the current weekly edition and
for the next day's issue, and also dealt with all current correspondence. The
day's issue showed no sign whatever of the calamity and it was not until the
12th October 1940 that an account appeared in the paper.

It was justly said: 'This destruction must have been greater but for the solid
walls, the work of another generation, which defended the fabric on Queen
Victoria Street. Windows indeed were smashed, the well-known clock disappeared, and there was some defacement, but the ancient red brick stood up
well to the test of modern bombardment. The partial ruin of neighbouring
structures showed how fierce the test had been.'

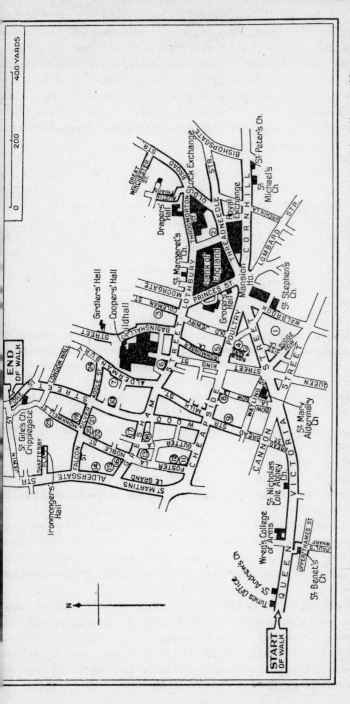

WALK 2. QUEEN VICTORIA STREET TO CRIPPLEGATE. 1. St. Antholin's Church Memorial. 2. Merchant Taylors' Hall. 3. St. Stephen's Church. 4. Simpson's Restaurant. 5. Mercers' Hall. 6. St. Laurence Jewry Church. 7. St. Mary-the-Virgin Church. 8. St. Mary-le-Bow Church. 9. Milton's birth-place. 10. St. Alban's Church. 11. Saddlers' Hall. 12. St. Vedast's Church. 13. Goldsmiths' Hall. 14. Aldersgate Site. 15. St. Anne's and St. Agnes's Church. 16. Ch⁴⁻ of St. John Zachary. 17. Haberdashers' Hall. 18. Waxchandlers' Hall. 19. Cooper's Arms. 20. Ch⁴⁻ of St. Olave. 21. Parish Clerks' Hall. 22. Coachmakers' and Coach Harness Makers' Hall. 23. Barbers' Hall. 24. Brewers' Hall.

For some time the accountants worked in the reel room and jobbing ware house, and leader writers found a spare office in the mechanical quarters.

The Prime Minister wrote to Lord Astor, the Chairman, congratulating him on the way the paper had carried on without a break. Lord Astor wa asleep in the board room when the bomb fell. Remarkable to relate, ther were hardly any casualties, and those were minor ones. All the clock stopped, but the Union Jacks waved as usual the following day over the hom of the great national newspaper.

A short distance east is the church of

ST. ANDREW-BY-THE-WARDROBE. This was a Wren church, com pleted in 1692. It had two side aisles, divided from the nave by square pillar encased in wood to the height of the galleries. The walls were wainscoted There was a richly coloured stained glass window, the gift of Samuel Wilson Lord Mayor, 1862; a well-carved pulpit with a sounding board, recently erected after lying for long in the vestry; two City Corporation pews adorned by the lion and the unicorn; a handsome sword-rest; and high-backed seat for churchwardens. There was also a somewhat remarkable monument, by the famous sculptor Bacon, to the Rev. William Romaine, thirty year rector, who died in 1795 at the age of eighty-one. An odd feature of it wa a figure of Faith pointing with a telescope. There was a tablet in memory o Henry Hennel, who was killed by an explosion at Apothecaries' Hall in 1842 The Apothecaries' Company gave a window dedicated to St. Luke in memory of a service held on the day of their patron saint.

The church has been burnt out but the tower remains. On the church floo there was left a stone recording the burial of two children—Eliza Atkinson daughter of James and Elizabeth Atkinson of Earl Street, Blackfriars, who died in 1789 at the age of nine months, and Thomas Atkinson, who died in 1791 at the age of twelve months.

The window and monument mentioned have gone. A monument tha remains, on the east wall, is that of a rector, Isaac Saunders, who died in 1836.

In the tower were three bells from Avenbury Church, Herefordshire dating from the fifteenth century. Of one of them there was a story that i had tolled of its own accord on the death of two vicars of Avenbury. The bell have probably survived. As it is dangerous to ascend the tower their condition is not known.

After passing on the north side Wren's College of Arms, which has sur vived intact, and on the south side a Wren Church, St. Benet's, Paul's Wharf also undamaged, there will be found the ruins of

ST. NICHOLAS COLE ABBEY CHURCH. There was a church her by the middle of the thirteenth century and restoration was carried out at the end of the fourteenth century. The church was burnt in the Great Fire and

Above (left). *The only ancient monument in St. Paul's Cathedral, that of John Donne. It was saved.* Right. *The monument to Jane Wren, daughter of Sir Christopher Wren.* Below. *The north transept before a bomb crashed on to it through the saucer dome, damaging the portico, monuments and glass*

Part of the nave of Austin Friars, which was longer than that of Winchester Cathedral. The church was more completely ruined than any in the City. Right. A service of commemoration held on the first anniversary of the German invasion of Holland, at which Queen Wilhemina of the Netherlands, Prince Bernhard, and the Dutch Premier, Dr. Gerbrandy were present

The brilliance of a bed of tulips contrasts with the blackened walls of ruined St. Bride's

Above. *The carving of the Last Judgment at St. Stephen's Church, Coleman Street, which was destroyed with the church.* Below. *The Roman roof tile with paw marks found with other Roman relics near Austin Friars when a building was being reinforced to withstand air raids*

rebuilt by Wren in 1677. It had a north and south aisle, panelled walls and Corinthian pilasters encased in wood. The stained glass over the reredos was the work of Burne-Jones.

It was reduced to a shell in the blitz and the upper part of the tower—shaped like a lighthouse in deference to the patron saint of seamen—was destroyed. Many of the treasures were lost, but the following survived: a chained commentary on the Prayer Book (1686); a fine old candelabrum; a sword-rest; an early sixteenth-century Spanish painting of the infant Jesus; a sixteenth-century lectern brought from Rome; a Flemish painting of the Madonna and Child (c. 1530).

On the north side, east of Cannon Street, is Watling Street. It leads to Budge Row where, at the corner of Sise Lane, was

ST. ANTHOLIN'S CHURCH MEMORIAL. This was an imposing monument of the Wren church demolished in 1874. There were two stone columns, with Corinthian capitals which supported an architrave and enclosed a medallion representation of the church. This has been destroyed but part of the tablet beneath, bearing an inscription, remains.

The reredos and other fittings from this church went to St. Antholin's, Nunhead Lane. The roof of the latter has been burnt off but the fittings had been removed for safety.

ST. MARY ALDERMARY, which is south of Watling Street, is one of Wren's few Gothic churches. It has sustained little damage.

South of the east end of Queen Victoria Street is

ST. STEPHEN'S CHURCH (Walbrook). This church, usually considered Wren's finest, was completed in 1679 (there have been churches on the site since the eleventh century). It was admired in the eighteenth century by the Earl of Burlington, a virtuoso, by John Wesley, and later by Canova, the Italian sculptor.

It has sustained damage in the blitz but happily not of a severe character. Whilst a huge hole was made in the dome, the main part of the fabric was not damaged. Restoration was carried out, and the church was reopened in 1944. The picture of the martyrdom of St. Stephen, on the north wall, was unharmed. The monuments—none of any special interest—are all intact. The vicar is Canon Gillingham, once a famous Essex cricketer.

North of St. Stephen's Church, Walbrook, is the

MANSION HOUSE. It was erected in 1739-53 as the first official residence of the Lord Mayor. It had two curious architectural excrescences at the top—one called 'Noah's Ark' and the other the 'Mare's Nest'. They were demolished respectively in 1795 and 1842. In its largest apartment, the Egyptian Hall, the Lord Mayor's banquet was held after the Guildhall was damaged. The Mansion House has suffered from a bomb in the vicinity, but not seriously.

East of the Mansion House is Cornhill. The two Wren churches here, St. Peter's (1681) and St. Michael's (1672), are undamaged. A few yards west of the latter is a memorial to the poet Gray.

At the east end of Queen Victoria Street is the

ROYAL EXCHANGE. The present building dates from 1844. Two previous ones were destroyed by fire. Slight damage was caused to the building in 1941 when a bomb fell on the subway to the Bank Tube Station. There were many casualties. Amongst the dead (they exceeded a hundred) was an old woman who had on her £900 in pound notes. No inquiries were made after her. The bomb here caused London's biggest crater and for a few weeks it was spanned by a bridge.

In Threadneedle Street, north of the Royal Exchange, are the ruins of the MERCHANT TAYLORS' HALL. The Company first occupied the site in 1331. The Hall was the largest of any City Company and was the only one with medieval features. After the Great Fire there was much rebuilding by Jarman but it still retained a crypt of 1375 and a great kitchen dating from about 1425. In the latter there were two enormous brick fireplaces, constructed at the end of the seventeenth century. The hall had stained glass, a minstrels' gallery, and a large buffet used occasionally for the display of the Company's magnificent plate. The great parlour, drawing-room and picture gallery contained seventeenth-century panelling. There was a small garden. The corridor and court room to which it led were built in 1878-9.

All that remains are the walls of the hall and reception rooms, with part of the offices. There were lost also busts of Queen Victoria, the Prince Consort, William Pitt, and Sir Robert Peel. All the portraits have survived, including those of Henry VIII, Charles I, two of Charles II, James II, William III, George III, Queen Charlotte, William Pitt, and Robert Dowe. The last was the donor of the sum of £50 to the parish of St. Sepulchre, Newgate, for a bell to be rung outside the condemned cell at Newgate to call its occupant to give heed to a summons to repent 'that you may not to eternal flames be sent.' The bell (perhaps the one referred to in Macbeth) is on exhibition at St. Sepulchre's Church. A monument to Dowe is in the Church of St. Botolph, Aldgate, where he was buried in 1612.

The Company's plate has been saved. This includes: the silver cloth-yard (before 1509); a mace (sixteenth century); silver parcel-gilt rosewater dishes (1590 and 1597); silver goblet (1631); silver caudle cup (1666); silver tankard (1666); silver-mounted ivory hammer (1679); silver gilt rosewater dish and ewer (1685); silver tumbler cup (1697) and a silver gilt monteith, or punch bowl (1700).

On the west side of Princes Street, which is west of the Bank of England, is GROCERS' HALL. The Company has been here since about 1427. The present Hall dates from 1893. It is a very fine apartment, and is approached by a noble staircase—hardly equalled in any other Hall. Both hall and stair-case are undamaged but a flying bomb destroyed some of the offices. At the foot of the staircase is a bell from the church of All Hallows, Staining, de-molished, except for the tower, in 1870. It bears the date 1458 and rang 'for joye of ye execution of ye Queene of Scots'.

In the court room are some ancient fittings. The overmantel to the fire-place is panelled and carved, and bears an inscription recording the benefac-tions of Sir John Cutler and Sir John Moore with three painted shields of arms.

Amongst the Company's plate is a coconut cup with gilt mounts (c. 1580), a gilt cup and cover (1672), and a tazza (1679). There is also a seventeenth-century Flemish carved wood figure of St. Anthony. The oldest document is a Grant of Land in Bucklersbury by Edward VI in 1548. '. . . Smell like Bucklersbury, in simple-time' says Falstaff in *The Merry Wives of Windsor*. Grocers and apothecaries at this time were combined.

There was little damage to the Bank of England.

Princes Street leads into Lothbury, on the north side of which is Coleman Street. Here, at the south end was

ST. STEPHEN'S CHURCH. It is known that there was a church on the site at the latest about 1214; there may have been rebuilding in medieval times. Burnt in the Great Fire, it was rebuilt by Wren. It was a plain building without aisles, measuring 75 ft. in length and 35 ft. in breadth. The oak pulpit was well carved. There was also an oak altar-piece with Corinthian pilasters. The communion table and the rails were particularly fine. In the vestry was an alto-relievo representing the Last Judgment. There were about a hundred figures, and Christ the Judge was on the throne, His right hand holding a small banner charged with a cross, His left the mundus—an emblem of sovereignty. Satan was beneath—in the descent to Hell. Angels were blow-ing trumpets, coffins were shown open, and risen bodies—some, those of children—were ascending to the clouds. This was destroyed with the church but a copy at the gateway, in plaster, is undamaged. The date 1780 is on the inside of the gate. A similar tablet is outside the churches of St. Giles-in-the-Fields and St. Andrew, Holborn (see p. 79).

East of Princes Street is the Wren

CHURCH OF ST. MARGARET (1690), which has sustained very little damage. Its principal feature is a screen composed of twisted columns, finely carved, surmounted by two eagles with two eaglets. It was given to the Church of All Hallows the Great (see p. 90) by the German merchants, Theodore and Jacob Jacobsen (who then resided in that parish), in the last years of the seventeenth or the first years of the eighteenth century. It also has a remarkably fine font, attributed to Grinling Gibbons.

AUSTIN FRIARS

This is north of the junction of Throgmorton and Old Broad Streets.

'Austin' is short for 'Augustine'. There was a church and priory of Augustinian friars here in 1253. In 1354 the church was rebuilt on a more elaborate scale. It was a place of important burials: Edmund Plantagenet, half-brother of Richard II (1371); Richard Fitzalan, Earl of Arundel (1397); John De Vere, 12th Earl of Oxford (1463)—an ancestor of Edward De Vere, the 17th Earl of Oxford (to an increasing number, including the writer, the real 'Shakespeare'); the Duke of Buckingham (1521). The last two were beheaded on Tower Hill and in the play, *Henry VIII*, Buckingham is seen going to execution.

The friars were disestablished by Henry VIII in 1538. In 1550 the nave of the church, after repairs at the expense of the Crown, was given by Edward VI to Dutch refugees. Queen Mary expelled the refugees in 1553 but they returned under Elizabeth in 1559.

The church was much damaged by fire in 1862 and completely restored in 1863-5. It continued to be the Dutch church in London. There, until 1940, some seventy or eighty Dutch people gathered Sunday after Sunday in a nave longer than that of Winchester Cathedral. They sang their Dutch hymns (sitting) and listened to a Dutch sermon. At a very long narrow table, with an equally long bench in front, the sacrament was administered each Good Friday.

With a floor space larger than that of any other City church (red curtains sheltered the central portion of the nave from draught), it was a fine specimen of Decorated Gothic architecture. Now, of all the City churches, it presents the most complete ruin. In October 1940 a land mine destroyed it, leaving only the outlines of three arches and the flat tombstone of a few of the Dutch fraternity.

There was an interesting ceremony at the old church shortly before the War. On 15th February 1939 a tablet inscribed 'in grateful remembrance of the life and works of Hugo Grotius, Father of international law', who died in 1645, was unveiled by the Earl of Athlone, Chancellor of London University. Speeches were delivered by the Rev. J. Van Dorp, minister of the church, and Lord Macmillan. The Lord Mayor, Lord Halifax, and Dr. Patijn, Netherlands Minister for Foreign Affairs, were also present. The tablet was only slightly damaged when the church was destroyed.

Erasmus lived for a time, in 1513, close to the church. A document bearing his signature was removed for safety. The plate was also saved. This includes a large alms dish of 1625, flagons and stand patens of 1635, and cups of 1669.

A curious external feature of the church was a greengrocer's stall tucked inside the railings. This appears to have survived.

After the Dissolution the eastern part of the church, comprising the transept, choir and tower, as also the whole of the conventual buildings, were granted, under letters patent, to Sir William Paulet, Lord Treasurer and afterwards Marquis of Winchester. Hence Winchester Street in the vicinity.

The premises of Western Union House are to-day on part of the Marquis's site. At the beginning of the War, with a view to air raids, the Western Union Telegraph Company decided to reinforce the basement to withstand the possible collapse of the superstructure. This involved the sinking and concreting of a number of shafts to support new steel girder framework. The foundation for the concrete was the London clay, 14 feet below the basement floor, or 24 feet below the street level, and during excavation many remains of Roman date came to light. Piles of blackened oak were found at the bottom of the course of what had probably been a northern branch of the Walbrook. In the blue clay was a mass of grasses and plants. The pottery included parts of basins and dishes of red Samian ware, two of which are stamped with the marks of potters who worked at La Graufesenque, in Gaul, in 70-90, and one of a third-century potter at Trèves. The earliest fragment was a black rim of Belgic pottery (pre-Roman type), some pieces of mica-coated ware similar to those made in a Roman potter's kiln nearer the mouth of the Walbrook, the remains of several large amphorae—one of which still bears the mark of the potter's thumb. A roof-tile, left to dry, bears the marks of the feet of animals—it is suggested those of a dog chasing a cat. This probably belonged to second-century London. The finial of a votive lamp and the rim of an incense-burner may have belonged to a local temple or have been part of a household shrine. A woman's long hairpin, in gold bronze alloy, was found with a nail of the same material. Other domestic objects unearthed were part of an engraved iron stylus, with one end pointed for writing on wax, part of a shoe, and a perfect tear-bottle. A saxon dagger blade was found near another Roman roof-tile.

Through the zeal of Mr. Terence Gould of the Western Union Telegraph Company, all the above relics of a by-gone London have been nicely arranged in a show-case in the entrance hall. They are open to inspection during ordinary office hours.

In Throgmorton Street, a little to the west of Austin Friars, is *DRAPERS' HALL*. The site of this Hall was purchased from Henry VIII in 1541. It had been occupied by the recently executed Thomas Cromwell, Earl of Essex. Of the erection of this house John Stow wrote most interestingly:

This house being finished, and having some reasonable plot of ground left for a garden, he caused the pales of the gardens adjoining to the north part thereof, on a sudden to be taken down; twenty-two foot to be measured forth right into the north of every man's ground; a line there to be drawn, a trench to be cast, a foundation laid, and a high brick wall to be built. My father had a garden there, and a house standing close to his south pale; this house they loosed from the ground, and bare upon rollers into my father's garden twenty-two foot ere my father heard thereof; no warning was given him, nor other answer, when he speake to the surveyors of that work, but that their master, Sir Thomas, commanded them so to do; no man durst go to argue the matter, but each man lost his land, and my father paid the whole rent, which was 6s. 8d. the year, for that half which was left. Thus much of mine own knowledge have I thought good to note, that the sudden rising of some men causeth them to forget themselves.

The Tudor Hall was burnt in the Great Fire. The next, designed by Edward Jarman, was rebuilt in 1774, after partial destruction, also by fire. The fourth Hall was erected in 1870. It has twenty-eight detached columns, each a monolith of polished Devonshire granite, with pilasters of the same material. The ceiling, coved and panelled, is supported by a series of colossal male terminal figures. There is a fine staircase of marble and alabaster.

The damage done to the Hall in the blitz was not of a serious character and it continued to be used. The garden (in the adjacent Throgmorton Avenue) was probably formerly that of Thomas Cromwell, and perhaps also of Stow Senr. To it the infant Thomas Macaulay was taken when he lived in Birchin Lane. Sir George Trevelyan wrote: 'To this dismal yard, containing as much gravel as grass, and frowned upon by a board of Rules and Regulations almost as large as itself, his mother used to convoy the nurse and the little boy through the crowds that towards noon swarmed along Cornhill and Threadneedle Street; and thither she would return, after a due interval, to escort them back to Birchin Lane.'

The plate of the Drapers' Company, which has survived, includes a cup (1578); voiding dish—used to clear fragments from table—(1658); ewer and dish (1674); voiding knife (1678); cup (1682); rosewater dish (1685); and a tazza—a shallow ornamental bowl—(1685). There have also survived portraits of Mary Queen of Scots, of her son, James I, and of Nelson.

CHEAPSIDE

Cheapside is approached from the Royal Exchange by way of Poultry.
SIMPSON'S RESTAURANT, south side No. 76 (Bird-in-Hand Court). This restaurant, where once 'a fish ordinary' of four courses could be had for two shillings, has been bombed out of existence.

On the north side, east of Ironmonger Lane was
MERCERS' HALL. The site has been occupied by the Company since 1414. The last Hall was said to have been designed by Wren but is now attributed to Jarman. Its front now forms part of the Swanage Town Hall.

The hall had high panelled wainscoting and a ceiling of ornamental stucco work, also a good screen. The large court room had panelling and Ionic pilasters. There was carving worthy of Grinling Gibbons, and a fine marble staircase. Alone amongst the companies the Mercers had a chapel. It represented the Hospital church of St. Thomas of Acon, built by the knights who were a religious and military Order similar to the Templars. The chapel had a beautiful reredos, oak panelled walls, and a black and white marble pavement.

All that now remains is the entrance doorway in Cheapside (it dates from 1879 and is carved with the Company's arms), part of the walling of the Hall, and the offices in Ironmonger Lane. Happily the portraits (that of Sir Thomas Gresham is by Holbein), the furniture, and the plate have survived. The principal items of furniture are a sixteenth-century arm-chair of oak, a seventeenth-century communion table, a pair of walnut chairs, and two gilt mirrors. All these came from Trinity Hospital, Greenwich. Amongst the plate is a gilt cup and cover, with hall-mark 1499. It is inscribed:

> *To elect the Master of the Mercers*
> *hither am I sent,*
> *And by Sir Thomas Leigh for the same intent.*

Another treasure is a silver-gilt wagon and tun, weighing 64 oz. (1554). There are also a spoon (1565), gilt beaker (1604), a cup (1616), salt-cellar (1618), trencher salt-cellar (1619), 'Buddha' spoon (1637), gilt salt-cellar (1638), and a cup (1650).

In April 1945, the Rt. Hon. Winston Churchill, Prime Minister, was admitted to the Livery of the Company, in the ruins of Mercers' Hall. Afterwards, in his livery gown, he walked to Grocers' Hall where he was entertained at a luncheon attended by representatives of most of the City Companies.

THE GUILDHALL is approached by King Street. It was built between 1411 and 1423 and was much restored, but not actually rebuilt, after the Great Fire. The porch was constructed in 1425. The front was reconstructed by George Dance the Younger in 1789. A flat roof, erected by Wren after the Great Fire, and intended to be temporary, remained until 1866 when Sir Horace Jones, the City Architect, constructed the open one.

The Guildhall suffered badly on the night of 29th December 1940. The fire spread from the neighbouring church of St. Lawrence Jewry. The roof was burnt off. The figures of Gog and Magog (1708), being entirely of wood, were soon reduced to ashes. Only two of a number of stained glass windows remain. One, on the south side, represents Sir William Walworth striking down Wat Tyler; the other, on the north side, shows Henry V and his Queen at the Guildhall; Whittington throwing bonds into the fire (an old myth); the boy Whittington, attended by the necessary but dubious cat, standing on a wharf watching the unloading of vessels. This window was the last in date. It was presented by Viscount Wakefield in 1931. Some damage was sustained by the monuments but it was slight save for that to Nelson and Wellington. The head of the figure of Neptune on the former, and the left hand on the latter, have gone.

The canopy on the south side of the Hall, and the medieval window (opened up in 1909) are unharmed. There remains also the tablet on the north side recording famous trials in the pre-Fire Hall such as those of Anne Askew (1547), the Earl of Surrey (1547), Lady Jane Grey (1554), Dr. Lopez (1594) and Dr. Garnett (1606).

The most beautiful room in the Guildhall has been entirely destroyed. This was known as the aldermen's court room. It was probably built in the early part of the seventeenth century and restored after the Great Fire. It was re-embellished in 1807. It was beautifully panelled and had a black marble chimney-piece. There were paintings over it and on the ceiling by Sir James Thornhill. The council chamber was also destroyed. This was erected in 1884 from the designs of Sir Horace Jones and therein was a tablet commemorating the previous chamber (1614) and Charles I's demand, in 1642, for the surrender of the five members of Parliament including John Hampden. The handsome brass gates have survived.

A piece of the charred roof timbers of the Guildhall has been carved by a London fireman to represent the façade of the building, and was presented by the National Fire Service Benevolent Fund to the International Association of Fire Fighters of America.

The Library dates from 1873 and is a fine building. Happily it has escaped the blitz. A stained glass window represents Richard De Bury (author of *Philobiblon*), the fourteenth-century Bishop of Durham; Richard Whittington; Sir Thomas Gresham; John Stow; and John Milton. Also such printers as Gutenberg, Caxton, Wynkyn de Worde, and Pynson. Sir George Frampton's fine bust of Chaucer was removed for safety.

Unfortunately, the books fared worse than the building. About 25,000 volumes were lost. The subjects were: London; standard works on history, biography, art, archaeology, genealogy, and local history; publications of antiquarian, archaeological, and other societies; calendars of state papers, rolls series, etc.; annuals, such as Court and City Calendars. Many of the damaged books were successfully treated by Zaehnsdorf (see p. 27). They were opened out on benches, tables, and chairs, and were subjected to gentle heat from coke fires for nearly two months. The famous Charter given to London by William the Conqueror (c. 1067) has been saved. Also the statues of Edward VI, Charles I, and his Queen, Henrietta Maria, which came from the front of the Guildhall Chapel. Most of the pictures in the badly damaged Art Gallery had been removed.

The Gallery has been re-opened, and in addition to some of the old pictures, there is the painting by Frank O. Salisbury of the Rt. Hon. Winston Churchill being presented with the freedom of the City at the Guildhall. It was commissioned by Sir Samuel Joseph, Lord Mayor in 1943, and presented to the Corporation by his widow and son in 1944. There also is a drawing described as 'A Prospect of the City of London from the south-east in the year 1945 showing its architecture, the destruction caused by the King's enemies during the previous five years and some of the means whereby the safety of the citizens was maintained'. Mr. Cecil Brown, the architect responsible, has appended the following:

This Drawing is dedicated by the Artist without permission to the Citizens of London who during five years withstood bombardment in various forms. 'You worked. From your needed efforts you would not be deterred. You carried on, and from your midst arose no cry for mercy, no wail of defeat. Your faith and endurance have finally been rewarded.'

The quotation is from General Eisenhower's speech at the Guildhall on 12th June 1946.

The early fifteenth-century crypt remains. In due course it will again house the City Corporation's most interesting museum. Meantime there is a small exhibition on and around the staircase leading to the Library; the entrance is in Basinghall Street. At the time of writing this includes a Viking gravestone, with Runic inscription, excavated in St. Paul's Churchyard in 1852; a missal from the Church of St. Botolph, Aldersgate; a register, dated 1538, from the Church of St. Mary Aldermanbury; the marriage register from St. Mildred's, Bread Street, open at 30th December 1816, to show the entry relating to Percy Bysshe Shelley and Mary Wollstonecraft Godwin. As there is so much to show, and so little space, the exhibits will be changed quarterly.

The medieval porch (c. 1425), in the vaulting of which are the arms of Edward the Confessor, and Henry VI, also the symbols of the four evangelists, has not been damaged.

East of Guildhall is Basinghall Street. Here on the east side was GIRDLERS' HALL. The Company has been here since 1431. The first Hall was destroyed in the Great Fire. The new Hall, erected in 1681, was enlarged in 1735, and restored and altered in 1878-9; there was further rebuilding in 1887. It had a fine old oak screen and gallery, a beautiful drawing-room and an overmantel containing a painting by Richard Wilson. There was a little walled garden which contained a lead cistern dated 1697, presented by a firm in Aldersgate Street.

The Hall was destroyed on 27th December 1940. A few things were saved: a famous Indian carpet made at Lahore, in 1634, at the factory of Akbar the Great, some silver, and the cistern. The minute books and glass were, however, sent to the Clothworkers' Hall and were there subsequently lost by

bombing. On the west side of Basinghall Street, in the Guildhall block, was
COOPERS' HALL. This Hall was built in 1868 on the same site as the first
one erected in 1547 and burned in the Great Fire. It had wood carving from
the previous building.

The Hall was badly damaged on 29th December 1940, the fire spreading
from the neighbouring Guildhall. The contents of the court room were
entirely destroyed. Amongst these was a portrait of Sir David Salomans, a
Jewish banker. In 1830 the City Council modified the theological termino-
logy of the oath to be taken on admission to the freedom, whereupon he
applied for membership of the Coopers' Company. He was admitted in July
1831, and in 1855 he became Lord Mayor (an event commemorated by a
stained glass window in the Guildhall until its destruction on the same night)
The Company took a large part in securing this honour for him. He was made
a baronet in 1869. Further portraits lost were those of Sir Felix Booth (Master
in 1831) and John Francis Firth (Master in 1847). A large leather screen and
the Master's chair were destroyed, in addition to a tablet commemorating
the Egham Charity founded in the early part of the eighteenth century by
Henry Strode of that town, who was Master in 1703, and a royal coat of arms
that was over the landing. There was also destroyed an elaborate wooden
mantelpiece with the arms of Charles II; this was a relic of the second Hall

The two oldest of the Company's pictures were saved by having been
taken to the basement. These were of Avice Gibson (who died in 1554), and
of her husband, Sir Anthony Knyvett. Another full-length likeness of the
former benefactor—painted for the Company in 1567—and a portrait, believed to be that of Henry Strode, were destroyed. There was saved a pall
chest, a bracket carved and gilded, and decorated with the Company's arms
(c. 1680), and the Company's plate. This includes a tankard (1649), a seventeenth-century German cup, and a tortoiseshell and silver snuff box (1701)

This is the only Company whose annals have been published during the
War: A Short History of the Worshipful Company of Coopers of London, by Sir
William Foster, 1944.

To the west of the Guildhall, in Gresham Street, is
ST. LAWRENCE JEWRY CHURCH. There was a church here—in the
Jewish quarter of London—in 1136. This may have lasted until the Great
Fire; there is no known rebuilding. Wren's church was completed in 1680
Only the church of St. Mary-le-Bow was more costly.

The church contained only one aisle, on the north side, and this was separated from the main body of the building by Corinthian columns. Above the
columns was a rich entablature, which was continued round the church, the
place of the columns being supplied on the south side by pilasters attached to
the walls. The ceiling was divided by projecting bands into sunken panels
and the plaster work with which it was adorned was excellently done. The

doorways, the organ case, the pulpit, and the font cover were all well carved. There was a modern stained glass window, in memory of Sir Thomas More who, about 1501, in the pre-Fire church, delivered a course of lectures on Augustine's *City of God*. As the Lord Mayor and Corporation attended here annually—on Michaelmas Day—before the election of a new Lord Mayor, there was a large square pew, displaying the arms of the City of London, in which was a fine sword rest, an arm-chair and a table.

It had the most beautiful vestry of any City church. The walls were encased with dark oak, handsomely carved, and over the chimney-piece there was a picture of the martyrdom of St. Lawrence on the gridiron (said to have taken place in Rome about A.D. 258), attributed to Spagnoletto (Ribera), who died in 1652. On the finely moulded ceiling there was a painting representing the translation of the martyr, the gridiron having been transformed into a harp.

The church was severely damaged on 29th December 1940. Mr. Douglas A. Clarke, churchwarden of St. Michael Bassishaw (one of the parishes united with that of St. Lawrence), gave a short account of the disaster in a news talk arranged by the B.B.C. Referring to the morning after the raid, he said:

Before going to the office I went to St. Lawrence Jewry hoping that it was safe. But it was desolate. The four stone walls stood fast and the masonry of Wren's square-built tower had withstood the fire; but the roof had collapsed and the whole church was knee-deep in smoking, smouldering ash and wreckage. . . .

Some of the great oak beams were still burning when I got there. They were alarmingly close to the strong room, built into the tower walls, where the ancient records and plate were stored. I asked a party of firemen for help. . . . They hacked away the burning timber and cooled the strong room door and walls with water from their hoses. Then came days of anxiety. When at last the strong room was opened the Church beadle entered. There was a moment of suspense, and then he handed out the treasures.

These included the plate, which could challenge comparison with that of any other City church. In addition to pre-Reformation communion vessels valued at £5,000, there are the following items from the church of St. Mary Magdalene, Milk Street (its site was Honey Lane Market; it was not rebuilt after the Great Fire): cup of 1548; cup and paten of 1561; cup of 1566; two flagons of 1633; seal-head spoon of 1638; two stand-patens of 1684; two silver-gilt dishes of 1684; cup of 1685. There are also, from the church of St. Michael Bassishaw in Basinghall Street (which was closed in 1893 and demolished in 1897): cup (c. 1600) with lid embossed with the figure of a soldier; stand-paten of 1629; flagon of 1629, with three small busts of women on the body of the vessel. Ribera's painting of St. Lawrence's martyrdom (during the

Great Fire it was rescued from the old church by a youth) was a second time saved. All that remained in the church were the sword-rest from the Lord Mayor's pew, and the nineteenth-century brass lectern eagle. The weather-vane gridiron (emblem of the martyrdom of St. Lawrence) fell into the old churchyard. It had probably never been down from the tower since it was erected. It measures 30 ins. by 27 ins. Some of the metal of the eight bells was recovered and a few of the stone monuments. Amongst the latter was that of Archbishop Tillotson, who died in 1694. It was cracked in several places. The destruction of the picture of Christ over the altar revealed the mosaic of the Ascension, introduced in 1867.

On a pillar in the ruins is a tablet with the following interesting inscription:

This Canadian ensign was presented to this Church by the Mayor of Vancouver, Mr. G. G. McGeer, K.C., M.P. as a memorial of a visit of the Rt. Hon. Lord Mayor of London, Sir Percy Vincent, to the City of Vancouver, B.C. on the occasion of the celebration of its golden jubilee year, and also to commemorate the visit in July 1936 of the Mayor of Vancouver to return thanks to the Lord Mayor, the Aldermen, and Sheriffs and the members of the Court of Common Council of the City of London for giving to the city of Vancouver a replica of the mace of London.

The ensign was destroyed.

The usual services were transferred to the church of St. Mary Woolnoth, Lombard Street. When, after two years' work, the church was in a safe state of repair, plans were made for the erection of a small chapel in the ruins. The space was found beneath the tower and this was enclosed and roofed in, affording accommodation for about twenty people. It was dedicated on 18th December 1943. The building and contents cost about £1,100. The oak pews and the marble and slate floor blocks were salved from the burnt Christ Church, Victoria Street, and were presented by the vicar and churchwardens there. The small windows, with coloured glass representations of St. Lawrence (with a figure of the burning church on his arm) and his gridiron, were designed by Mr. Christopher Webb. A service bell of 3 cwt. was presented by Mr. A. A. Hughes, of Messrs. Mears and Stainbank, the Whitechapel bell foundry which cast it, and which claims to be the oldest firm in London; it was founded in 1570. The inscription on the bell is *Ecce post ignem vox* (After the fire a voice).

There was again some damage—to glass—by a flying bomb on 25th July 1944. In commemoration, a silver wafer-box was presented by Lady Scott, Superintendent of the City Centre of the Women's Voluntary Services (Civil Defence) in King Street, 'in thanksgiving for the preservation of the members from harm by a flying bomb on 15th July 1944'.

The most recent addition is the font (1620), which was saved from what was once the Church of Holy Trinity, Minories (see p. 98).

North-west of the Guildhall is Aldermanbury. Here is the church of *ST. MARY THE VIRGIN*. There was a church on the site in 1148. It was rebuilt in the fifteenth century, destroyed in the Great Fire, and again rebuilt by Wren in 1677. It included two side aisles, divided from the main body of the church by composite columns, There was a small tablet in memory of the infamous Judge Jeffreys. As he had been a parishioner, his body was dis-interred from the Tower of London and buried here in 1693.

The church has been reduced to a shell; an ancient chest, the font, and the altar-piece have all gone. The altar-piece displayed a picture of the Last Supper, by Franck, presented in 1777. It is believed that the tablet to Jeffreys was saved.

A small figure of the Virgin and Child over the doorway is intact. Also quite untouched is a bust of Shakespeare in the churchyard. The lengthy in-scription on this records that Heminge and Condell, the putative parents of the First Folio (1623), were parishioners. The bust has no resemblance to that on the Stratford monument, or to the portrait in the First Folio.

Returning to Cheapside, on the south side is found *ST. MARY-LE-BOW CHURCH*. There was a church on the site soon after the Norman Conquest—perhaps earlier. No doubt there was restoration but there was no known rebuilding before 1680, when it was necessitated by the destruction of the earlier church in the Great Fire. Wren spent more upon this church than upon any other, the total cost being £15,400. It was almost square, measuring 65 ft. by 63 ft. The interior was handsome. The two side aisles were separated from the main body by two Corinthian columns. These, with the entablature, supported an arched ceiling divided into panels and adorned with foliage and rosettes. There was a richly gilded altar-piece enclosed by Corinthian pillars: it was set up in 1706. The centre painting was a copy of Murillo's *Holy Family* (1913). The pulpit was of carved oak and had a monogram 'C.C.' representing Charles II and his Queen Catharine.

It had the most extensive crypt of any City church. The nave was 48½ ft. by 26½ ft., and the north aisle was of equal length and 14½ ft. wide. The south aisle, now sealed up, is of the same width and extends further westward. The three stone columns now visible in the nave are circular, with moulded bases and cushion capitals, and square moulded abaci; one capital is modern. One of these Norman cushion capitals has the carving of a spearhead—said to be unique in Europe. There are signs of Roman as well as of Saxon work.

The church has been reduced to a shell. The pulpit has been saved. The paintings mentioned have been destroyed, as also the font and all the bells; eight of them were re-cast twelve or fourteen years ago.

THE BELLS OF BOW

I cannot hear the bells of Bow
  That rang in town so long
And gave to London long ago
  A Cockney cradle-song.

But I can see the dragon still
  Upon the topmost spire
Who keeps his ancient domicile
  Despite his trial by fire.

He saw the City streets ablaze,
  The streets he knew so well,
He saw below a twisted maze
  Of buildings but a shell.

The bells of Bow we may not hear
  Until more tranquil days
But though the landmarks disappear
  The Cockney spirit stays.

HAROLD ADSHEAD

After the bombing there was discovered a tile-paved chamber below the floor level, south of the altar-piece and approached by stone steps, with the base-stone of a late Gothic door jamb at the bottom. It is possible it was part of a baptistry.

The only monument of any importance has survived. It was on the west wall and was that of Newton, Bishop of Bristol and later (1768) Dean of St. Paul's Cathedral. He edited Milton's *Paradise Lost* in 1749.

All the registers have been saved, including those brought from the Church of All Hallows, Bread Street. One of these contained the baptismal entry of John Milton (1608). A memorial window to the poet has been destroyed but on the outside of the west wall is still a tablet brought from All Hallows' Church. It bears Dryden's lines, prefixed to Tonson's folio edition of *Paradise Lost* (1688):

Three poets in three distant Ages born.
Greece, Italy, and England did adorn;
The First in Loftiness of Thought surpasst,
The Next in Majesty—in both the last;
The force of Nature could no further go;
To make a third she joined the other Two.

In the Kit-Cat portrait of Tonson in the National Portrait Gallery he is shown holding in his hand a copy of this edition of *Paradise Lost*.

The fine steeple of the church (221 ft. high) remains—surmounted by the City dragon, nearly nine feet in length. The crypt is unharmed.

King Street, on the north side of Cheapside, leads to the Guildhall (see p. 53).

On the south side is a section of Bread Street. Here, in 1608, John Milton was born. A tablet to his memory which bore a medallion of the poet and was erected on the site of All Hallows' Church, where he was baptized, has disappeared. The church was demolished in 1878.

On the north side of Cheapside, a little farther west, is Wood Street. At its north end is the ruined

ST. ALBAN'S CHURCH. This was a Wren church, completed in 1685. It had been much altered. The east window was replaced by three smaller ones. There was a well-carved pulpit, but with no sounding board. It had on it a frame for an hour-glass (to measure the length of sermons), but the latter had been removed to the vestry. There was a fine Elizabethan table and a marble font (1684).

The church was destroyed on 29th December 1940. Mr. H. L. Davies (son of the deceased vicar, the Rev. G. Sevier Davies), wrote,

The wooden screen and carved pulpit, with the hour-glass stand, were destroyed. The hour-glass itself, with the church plate, was in the safe in the tower, and I was not able to get in for a week owing to burning timber falling from the tower. Then, after scraping away six inches of hot ashes, I opened the safe and we found the hour-glass and plate, black but intact, in their wooden cases, the glue of which had dried so that the boxes fell apart, but there was no real damage done there. The four oldest registers were fortunately on loan and the other old ones, written on paper, were charred at the edges only. The ones on parchment were shrunk into small solid blocks, about one-sixth of the size of the covers and neither the British Museum nor the Record Office can do anything for them.

The altar paintings remain: Christ holding a mundus; Christ the Good Shepherd; Christ the Bread of Life.

As a result of the bombing, a blocked-up late Gothic doorway was found in the south wall.

In Cheapside, between Foster Lane and Gutter Lane, was

SADDLERS' HALL. The Company has been on the site certainly since the fourteenth century, and possibly earlier. The last Hall was erected in 1822 after a fire; the buildings in front dated from 1863-4. It has been entirely destroyed save a mere fragment of the entrance doorway.

There were some fittings from the previous Hall and a fine funeral pall (c. 1500). This has been saved, as also have charters of James I and Charles II. A charter of Queen Elizabeth (1558) has been destroyed.

All the Company's plate has been saved. This includes: a coconut cup (1627); silver-gilt loving cups (1651 and 1661); and a richly chased tankard (1676). There has also survived a ballot box bearing date 1619: it has been in regular use ever since for the annual election of wardens.

In Foster Lane (north) is

ST. VEDAST'S CHURCH. The earliest mention of a church here is about 1170. It appears to have been rebuilt in about 1519 and was repaired and 'beautified' in 1614. It was rebuilt after the Great Fire, in 1697-8, mostly upon the old walls. It is a small church, measuring 69 ft. by 21 ft. It includes a south aisle, separated from the main body of the church by arches supported on four Tuscan columns. It had a very handsome altar-piece with four Corinthian columns, and carvings of pelican, cherubim, urns, palm branches, etc. The pulpit and sounding-board were also well carved.

It has been badly damaged by bombs and most of the woodwork mentioned has gone. The building as a whole is not beyond reconstruction. It has still its most graceful steeple.

Mr. Edward Yates reports the discovery of 'a Gothic blocked-up doorway in the south wall, clearly showing, as elsewhere, that Wren made use of the lower part of the walls of the earlier church if they were sound'.

Farther down the Lane is

GOLDSMITHS' HALL. The site has been occupied since the early fourteenth century. In the Great Fire an early fifteenth-century Hall was partly destroyed, but there were some remains of medieval work until its demolition in 1829. The rebuilding, by Philip Hardwick, was completed in 1835. Its façade is as imposing as that of the Fishmongers' Hall but it is unfortunately much more congested. It has some magnificent rooms and the court diningroom, with its Corinthian pillars, panelled ceiling, huge chandeliers, and portrait-covered walls, was a fine sight on the occasion of the dinner held at the Trial of the Pyx—the testing of the newly minted coinage. The drawingroom and court dining-room were completely destroyed. There was also damage to the livery hall and court room, but they were rendered usable. The Assay Office in Gutter Lane was entirely destroyed in 1940. Thereafter hall-marking was carried out at Goldsmiths' Hall.

One of the treasures of the Hall (all of which have been saved) is a small altar to Diana in the court room. This was discovered when digging the foundations. There is also a finely carved figure of St. Dunstan. His head bears a large mitre and in his left hand is a long pastoral staff. It came from the Company's barge. There is a carved cartouche bracket with the date 1669, and seventeenth-century panelling with an enriched cornice from East Acton Manor House.

The Goldsmiths' Company has probably a finer collection of plate than any other Company. The following are a few of the items: cressener cup (1503); the Bowes cup (1554)—Queen Elizabeth drank from this at her coronation; she then presented it to Sir Martin Bowes as his fee cup for acting as butler, and he presented it to the Company; a ewer (1574); the Myddelton cup (1599)—it was given by the Company to Sir Hugh Myddelton in recog-

When the fine interior of St. Lawrence Jewry (left) with its rich carving and plaster work, was destroyed, there was revealed a mosaic of the Ascension (right) which had been covered by the picture over the altar

The vestry of St. Lawrence Jewry (left), more beautiful than that of any City church, and the most handsome apartment in the Guildhall, the Aldermen's Court Room, which were both destroyed

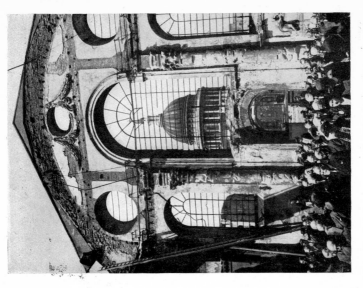

St. Mary-le-Bow, Wren's costliest church, with its beautifully decorated ceiling, richly-gilded altar-piece and slender Corinthian columns, is now only a shell. The famous Bow bells were destroyed with it

The spire of St. Mary-le-Bow (left) and the towers of St. Mary Aldermary, and (extreme right) St. Mildred, Bread Street, seen across the wilderness of flowering weeds which rapidly covered some of the scars left by the bombing of the city

nition of his completion of the New River Scheme (1613); the Company acquired it in 1922; grace cups (1616 and 1619); tankard (1661) with the inscription 'This potte was made of ye silver of ye canopie when King Charles ye 2nd was crowned April 23 1661'; tankard (1683) and porringer (1689).

West of Cheapside is

ST. MARTIN'S-LE-GRAND. The General Post Office, on the west side, has been practically destroyed down to the first floor.

St. Martin's-le-Grand leads to

ALDERSGATE STREET

The building (No. 62) bearing the City Corporation plaque marking the site of Aldersgate is intact. A short distance beyond is the Church of St. Botolph without Aldersgate, which has not been damaged.

At the south end of Aldersgate Street is Gresham Street, and here, on the left, is

ST. ANNE'S AND ST. AGNES'S CHURCH. It was completed by Wren in 1681. It is built of brick and is only 53 feet square. Its features were Corinthian columns, walls panelled with oak to the height of 8½ feet, a high gilded altar-piece, and an east window with some good stained glass. There were no important monuments.

The church has been badly damaged but not beyond repair.

A short distance beyond a churchyard at the corner of Noble Street, which has been pleasingly laid out since the blitz (it is that of St. John Zachary, the church of which was not rebuilt after the Great Fire) is the site of

HABERDASHERS' HALL. It was bequeathed to the Company by William Baker in 1478. The last Hall dated from 1864. The court room had a good plaster ceiling and a seventeenth-century oak screen of five bays. All this has been destroyed.

The portraits, including one by Gainsborough and two by Reynolds, and the plate have been preserved. The latter includes a gilt salt cellar (1595); a gilt loving cup, repoussé with scenes from *The Book of Tobit* (1629); wine goblet (1634); gilt loving cup (1637); wine goblet (1648); flagon (1670); and a tankard (1672). A carved cabinet bearing a list of benefactors, an eighteenth-century 'Parliament clock', and the figure-head, representing St. Catherine, which belonged to the Company's barge, have also survived, though the pennant of the last was destroyed. Items lost were: a small figure of Henry VIII; two carved festoons of fruit and flowers from door-heads, one with a cartouche of the Company's arms; and some sixteenth-century panelling from Pitley Manor House.

Opposite the site of the Haberdashers' Hall was the

WAXCHANDLERS' HALL. This site has been owned by the Company at the latest since 1493. The post-Fire Hall was demolished in 1852 and a small Hall erected from designs by C. Fowler.

After the blitz the ground floor and basement alone remained. The silver, charters, muniments, and some of the more valuable furniture and portraits were saved, but much was lost.

Returning to Aldersgate Street, at No. 33 is Shaftesbury Place. Here is the *IRONMONGERS' HALL.* This is a modern 'Tudor' building, opened in 1925. It is the most recent of the Companies' Halls, and was erected in consequence of the previous Hall (in Fenchurch Street) having been destroyed in a daylight bombing raid on 7th July 1917. In the recent war it sustained trivial damage, which was soon repaired. Outside is a figure of St. Lawrence bearing his gridiron; also one of St. Eligius. He lived in the seventh century and is regarded as the patron saint of blacksmiths and workers in metals. He was by trade a goldsmith, and used his craft to make vessels for the church when he became Bishop of Noyon. Once, as a smith, it is said, he was shoeing a horse which, being possessed by the devil, kicked so furiously that no one dare touch it. The saint cut off its leg, put on the shoe, and then, with the sign of the cross, joined the leg on again!

After retracing steps for about a hundred yards, Falcon Street is reached. The board a little way down that turning, on the site of the Coopers' Arms, is a reminder that the destroyed tavern bore a City Corporation plaque indicating that in a house on its site William Shakspere lived in 1604. This discovery (of no importance to those who regard him as only an actor) was the result of the researches of an American, Professor Wallace, published in *Harper's Magazine* in March 1910. Opposite is the churchyard of St. Olave. The church was not rebuilt after the Great Fire.

At the east end of Falcon Street is Silver Street and in this thoroughfare (on the south side) was the

PARISH CLERKS' HALL. The Company came to this site after the Great Fire; the Hall was erected c. 1669. It was seriously damaged by fire in 1765 and subsequently enlarged and repaired. The front was modern; the lower part of the building was let as offices.

The Hall has been destroyed. The Company has lost some old portraits and other treasures, such as the Master's Chair (c. 1690); a brass candlestick (seventeenth century); Warden's chair (eighteenth century); clock given in 1786; beadle's staff head (1789); and a snuff box made from wood of the *Victory*.

There have been saved a book containing a Bede-roll from 1236; a Book of Mortality (1581-2); a pall of about 1500—restored 1686; a Grant of Arms (1582); a tankard, engraved with Chinese decoration (1682); and a tobacco box (1691).

The Parish Clerks' is not a Livery Company.

In Noble Street, which runs south from the junction of Falcon Street and Silver Street, was the

COACHMAKERS' AND COACH HARNESS MAKERS' HALL. The Company has occupied the site since 1703, the Hall being then taken over from the Scriveners. Great alterations were made in 1841-3, and the Hall was rebuilt 1867-70.

The Hall, which had an oak screen and good panelling, has been entirely destroyed but the Company has saved most of its treasures. These include a loving cup (1650); gilt flagon (1680); poor box (1680); two-handled porringer (1688); tankard (1688); silver-gilt flagon (1693); and the original model from which the royal state coach was made for George III and Queen Charlotte. It was designed by Sir William Chambers and painted by Cipriani. Amongst the losses were a Flemish cabinet of carved oak(1606) and the Master's Chair (1670).

In Monkwell Street, which turns north from Silver Street, was the *BARBERS' HALL.* The Barbers first erected a Hall on this site in 1381. In 1540, by statute, they were incorporated with the Surgeons. Holbein painted a picture depicting the king granting a charter: it was therefore symbolical rather than literal in truth. (There is an engraving of this picture dated 1736; one is in possession of the Clerk.) In 1636 Inigo Jones built a court room which later became the hall. It had a flat ceiling, ornamented richly, with a central oval opening surrounded by a deep curb of plaster foliage, fruit, and flowers. The spandrels were similarly adorned and on one of them were the Arms of the City. It was perhaps the most beautiful room to be seen in any of the Companies' premises. It had been the Barbers' Hall since 1745 when the Company, again by statute, was separated from the Surgeons.

The hall and the other apartments have been entirely destroyed. The Holbein picture—hidden during the War of 1914-18 under Trafalgar Square —was again removed in 1939, this time to the National Library of Wales (Aberystwyth). There were also saved by removal portraits of Charles II, Queen Anne, and Inigo Jones. The last was by Van Dyck.

All the plate has been saved, including 'a gilt cup given by King Henry VIII to this Company, with bells hanging at it, which every man is to ring by shaking after he hath drunk up the whole cup', thus described by Pepys (27th February 1663). Its hall-mark is 1523; it was presented in 1540. There is also a rosewater ewer (1657) and a silver-gilt cup and cover, the last presented in 1676 by Charles II. The trunk of the royal oak forms its handle, and the branches of the tree, from which hang gilt acorns, the cup itself; the cover is the royal crown. Another treasure is a large silver bowl (1704); it was presented by Queen Anne.

A continuation of Silver Street is Addle Street, and here was

BREWERS' HALL. There was a Hall on the site in 1420. It was rebuilt, as a result of the Great Fire, in 1673, and repaired in 1828. In 1875 the houses in front were rebuilt, and then formed a quadrangle. The hall was wainscoted—as an inscription on a medallion said, at the expense of Sir Samuel Starling, Lord Mayor, in 1670. There was a fine old fireplace, and its surround had on the pediment the crest of a Saracen woman, part of the Company's original crest. This referred to the old story that Thomas à Becket's mother met his father in Palestine and followed him to London, where she called out 'Gilbert, Gilbert' until she found her man. Dickens founded a purple passage upon this in his *Child's History of England*. It is assumed that, in some way, St. Thomas of Canterbury was of assistance to the Company and possibly he was its patron saint. There was a court room with porthole windows. There were also old-fashioned kitchens with wide fireplaces and spits.

The Hall has been destroyed, but some treasures have survived. Amongst these is a book kept by the Clerk, 1418-40; the charters, 1438, 1560, 1563, 1641, 1660 and 1685; a pall dated about 1500; and some barge banners.

CRIPPLEGATE

Wood Street crosses the junction of Silver Street and Addle Street and, by way of the northern half of the first-named thoroughfare the reader can reach the Church of

ST. GILES, CRIPPLEGATE. This church was rebuilt after a fire in 1545. It was a good specimen of the Perpendicular style, including a nave, chancel, and two side-aisles which were separated from the central portion by clustered columns and pointed arches. It was 146 ft. 3 in. in length. In 1791 a beautiful east window was installed; it had cherubs' heads after Sir Joshua Reynolds, who is said to have found his model in a daughter of the ranger of Green Park. There was a finely carved pulpit.

The church is associated with two great Englishmen: Oliver Cromwell and John Milton. Cromwell was married here in 1620. Milton's father was buried here in 1647; the poet in 1674. In 1793 the celebrated sculptor Bacon made a bust of John Milton which was placed against a pillar near the grave, and in 1862 the bust was removed to the north-east corner and placed on a cenotaph of Caen stone. In 1904 a full-sized statue was erected outside the church; the plinth was carved with a scene from *Comus* and the expulsion from Eden from *Paradise Lost*. The head was designed from the bust in Christ's College, Cambridge.

The church was subjected three times to attacks from the air. It was the first church to be hit—on 24th August 1940. It is now nothing but a ruin. Happily, the Milton bust was preserved in the crypt of the Church of St. Mary-le-Bow; the cenotaph remains, still showing the sculptured serpent and the flaming sword on its front. The statue outside was knocked off the plinth, and was subjected to some ignominious treatment. Once a tin hat was found upon its head; on another occasion it was missing and found in the churchyard holding an offertory bag and a bunch of keys, perhaps to illustrate the lines in *Lycidas*:

> Two massy keys he bore of metals twain
> (*The golden opes, the iron shuts amain*).

At last it was placed under the tower where, somewhat begrimed, it still is at the time of writing. A tablet commemorating Milton's place of burial has been destroyed.

The east window has entirely disappeared. Fragments of a few of the many monuments are left. That of Martin Frobisher, who was buried here in 1594, has lost its Elizabethan galleon and the lines from Macaulay's *Lay of the Spanish Armada*. John Speed's monument (he was buried here in 1629) has lost the bust and the accompanying book and skull. Constance Whitney (grand-daughter of Sir Thomas Lucy of Shakespearean lore) died in the same year. Her monument showed her rising from a coffin. The story was that the sexton, desiring to obtain a valuable ring, cut the finger of the supposed corpse, in an endeavour to remove it, whereupon she awoke from a trance and thus was saved from being buried alive. It was added that she returned home, married and had several children. This, however, could not be reconciled with the epitaph which stated that she died at the early age of seventeen years! There is no doubt that what the sculptor meant to represent was Constance rising at the sound of the last trump. Coffin and lady have gone but some part of the tablet remains (see p. 127). Richard Smyth, who died in 1675, had a monument that has sustained little damage. He was a famous book collector and the author of an 'Obituary' which dealt with personal recollections of people known to him between 1627 and 1674.

Two monumental tablets remain almost, if not quite, unimpaired:

1. Charles Langley, who died in 1602. The epitaph is still complete:

> If Langlie's life thou liste to knowe reade on and take a viewe
> Of Faith and Hope I will not speake his work shall shew them trew,
> Whoe whilest he lived, wth counsaile grave, ye better sorte did guid
> A stay to weake, a staffe to poore w^thout back-bite or pride,
> And when he died he gave his mite all that did him befall
> For ever once a yere to cloath Saint Giles his poore withall
> All Saintes hee pointed for the day gownes XX redie made
> With XX shirts and XX smockes as they may best be hadd,
> A sermon eke he hath ordayned that God may have his praiese,
> And others might be wonne thereby to followe Langlie's waies,
> On Vicar and Churchwardens then his truste he hath reposed,

As they will answer him one day when all shall be disclosed,
Thus, being deade, yet still he lives, lived never for to dye
In heaven's blysse, in worlde's fame and so I trust shall I.
                    Lanncellott Andrewes, Vicar
        John Taylor, Wm. Hewett, Edward Sicklyn, Richard Maye,
                            Churchwardens.

Lancelot Andrewes, who died in 1626 as Bishop of Winchester (there is a fine monument in Southwark Cathedral), was vicar of this church for seventeen years.

2. Thomas Stagg. This is a tablet bearing the simple inscription:

> *Thomas Stagg*
> *Attorney at Law*
> *Vestry Clerk of the Parish*
> *From the 16th day of March 1731*
> *to the 19th day of February 1772*
> *On which day he died*
> *That is all.*

There has been some discussion as to the meaning of the last three words. Were they meant satirically or did the donor thus tersely reply to the inquiry of the monumental mason as to whether he wanted nothing more in the inscription than the record of forty-one years as a parish clerk?

A memorial tablet that has entirely disappeared was a long one on the west wall to John Foxe, the author of *Actes and Monuments of these latter and perilous times touching matters of the Church,* the short title of which is *The Book of Martyrs.* He was buried here in 1587. There was also a tablet to Richard Busby (1575) with a long inscription like Langlie's. Another with an odd inscription was to Edmund Harrison

who, having lived above 40 yeeres a batcheloar, had to wife Jane, ye eldest daughter of
Thomas Godfrey, late of Hodiford, in ye county of Kent, Esqr., by whom he had issue twelve
sonnes and nine daughters, of wich at ye time of his death were only living three sonnes,
Godfrey, Edmund, and Peter, and 2 daughters, Sarah and Jane. He was embroiderer to
3 Kings, viz. King James, King Charles 1st and King Charles 2nd, lefte ye troubles of this
world ye 9th day of January 1666, in ye 77 yeare of his age in a christian assurance of a
resurrection unto life eternall, to who's memorie his eldest sonn Godfrey erected this monument.

ST. GILES CRIPPLEGATE

The silence of deserted aisles
Hangs as a pall about St. Giles;
Oh! strange and yet prophetic fate
That named this parish Cripplegate;
Yet time has shown how Cowper's curse
A long while since expressed in verse,

'Ill fare the hands that heaved the stones'
For all who would disturb the bones,
Has brought a Nemesis of doom
To those who threatened Milton's tomb;
Here Frobisher brought home from Brest
And reverently laid at rest,
Saw London made a vast redoubt
And new Armadas put to rout,
Here Foxe within the chancel near
Saw yet another reign of fear,
And he could write a Martyr's Book
How London's heroes undertook
By many a brave and noble act
To keep the ancient faith intact;
Here Speed with book and skull in hand
For long historian of our land
May dream of writing once again
Of war and death; of grief and pain;
His memory will still inspire
Recorders of the later Fire,
Milton Frobisher Foxe and Speed,
Famous in act and word and deed,
Have gone to their eternal sleep
But still their legacies we keep;
So from these aisles where rubble lies
St. Giles in pride again will rise.

HAROLD ADSHEAD

The font (c. 1858) was badly damaged. From it, in the ruins, the grand-daughter of the last verger was christened in 1941. A lectern, given in 1888 in memory of Lancelot Andrewes, is preserved, as also are two sword-stands. The vestry, too, remained intact. All the registers had been carefully preserved at Cripplegate Institute, a short distance west of the church. Apart from the entries of Cromwell's marriage and Milton's burial, they are most interesting in view of the terrible mortality caused in this parish by the Great Plague. In one day, 18th August 1665, 263 burials were recorded.

The entrance doorway, which has survived, dates from 1903. The figure is that of the patron saint, St. Giles. He is represented with a hind as, according to tradition, one took refuge in the saint's cave when pursued by dogs. The animal, in return, provided its deliverer with milk. St. Giles (he was born in Athens but went to live in France about 666) is the patron saint of maternity as well as of the poor and needy, but 'Cripplegate' probably derives from an Anglo-Saxon word meaning a burrow or covered way.

The tower of the church has survived. It was raised sixteen feet, between 1682 and 1684. There was a fine carillon of bells, set up in the tower in 1794. It was arranged to play at 9 a.m., 1, 3 and 9 o'clock, the tunes being: Sunday, 'the Easter Hymn'; Monday, 'God save the King'; Tuesday, 'Auld Lang Syne'; Wednesday, the 'Tune Hanover'; Thursday, 'Caller Herrin'; Friday 'The Mariners' Hymn'; Saturday, 'Home Sweet Home'. The bells were re-hung in 1908, two being recast. Four of the twelve bells melted away in the fire; the remaining eight are so badly cracked that they must be recast.

After the bombing the vicarage, a little to the south of the church, was so badly damaged that it was demolished.

The bastion of the Roman wall still remains in the churchyard. Another, discovered through the bombing, much restored by modern brickwork but showing some medieval remains, is illustrated in this book.

Close to the church was for some two years an allotment. It was made of earth brought by the Anti-Fire Service from Hampstead Heath.

Walk 3

Newgate Street ★ Smithfield ★ Holborn ★ Theobald's
Road ★ Bloomsbury ★ Tottenham Court Road

NEWGATE STREET

is north of St. Paul's Cathedral.

It has a big gap on the south side, and from this point a fine view of St.
Paul's Cathedral, quite unprecedented, can be obtained; on its right is the
tapering leaden spire of the Church of St. Martin, Ludgate. Up to the beginning of the War, on the north side, near St. Martin's-le-Grand, there was a
stone tablet showing figures of William Evans, Charles I's giant porter, and
Sir Geoffrey Hudson, a dwarf who figures in Scott's *Peveril of the Peak*.
Hudson was once served in a pie for the amusement of King Charles I and
his Queen, Henrietta Maria, and was sometimes put in the pocket of Evans.
The tablet has disappeared.

At the east end of the north side is

CHRIST CHURCH, NEWGATE. This was a Wren church built (1687)
on the site of the old church of the Greyfriars. It was rather a fine building.
On each side of the middle aisle was a colonnade of six bays with composite
columns and pilasters on responds standing on high square bases. Above was
a plastered timber clerestory, panelled at the base and having a segmented-
headed window in each bay, supported on each side by a rich plaster scroll
encircling a cherub's head, and with festoons of fruit and flowers. There was
a good reredos with Corinthian columns, and panelled wainscoting round
the walls. Outside the sanctuary was some paving from the Greyfriars'
Church (c. 1360). There was a well-carved pulpit: it was brought from the
Temple Church about 1839. The stalls were modern but there was some old
panelling, said to have come from a ship of the Spanish Armada.

The gravestone of James Boyer, the master immortalized by Charles Lamb
in his essay, *Christ's Hospital Five and Thirty Years Ago*, was within the altar
rails. He died in 1814. In 1924 a tablet was installed in memory of Richard
Baxter who was buried here in 1691. In 1932 William Temple, then Archbishop of York, later Archbishop of Canterbury, unveiled a tablet in memory
of Lawrence Shyrfe, founder of Rugby School. He was buried here (1567)
although his wish was to be interred at Rugby.

The church has always been closely associated with Christ's Hospital,

F

which removed to Horsham in 1902. The high pews of the 'Grecians' (boys intended for the University) remained in the galleries and annually, on St. Matthew's Day (21st September), about three hundred boys came up to hear a sermon by an old blue. Coleridge was a 'Grecian': Lamb and Leigh Hunt were less exalted. In 1935 the late Lord Plender unveiled a bust of Lamb which was placed in a niche outside the church. It was inscribed:

> *Elia.*
> *To the immortal memory of*
> *Charles Lamb*
> *Perhaps the most loved name in English*
> *literature who was a Blue-coat boy here for*
> *7 years.*
> *B.1775.*   *D.1834.*

The church has been reduced to a shell; all the pews have gone. The pulpit and the font-cover have been saved. Boyer's tombstone remains, though it is cracked in several places. Also, in part, can be seen the gravestone of Richard Roystone 'Bookseller to three Kings', who died in 1686 at the age of eighty-six, and Thomas Hollies, a 'chirurgeon', who died in 1690. There has also survived the memorial to the Rev. Samuel Crowther, vicar, who died in 1829. In the vestibule was a small tablet brought from the cloisters of Christ's Hospital when it was demolished in 1902. It reads:

> *Here Lyes*
> *A BENEFACTOR*
> *Let no one*
> *Move his Bones.*

This tablet has survived, but the benefactor's wishes have not been observed His remains—those of James St. Amond, who died in 1754—were removed on the demolition of the school, to the City Corporation Cemetery at Ilford

The tablets in memory of Baxter and Shyrfe have been destroyed. The Lamb bust was, marvellously, preserved, and was removed to Christ's Hospital.

A rest room, which Mr. E. S. Underwood, F.R.I.B.A., the Church architect, had erected for the vicar, was unharmed. All the plate has been saved. This includes: cup and cover patens of 1560, 1562, 1592, and 1616 respectively (the last given to the Church of St. Leonard, Foster Lane, which was not rebuilt after the Great Fire); two patens of 1616; stand paten of 1617; silver dish of fine pierced Indian work with a scalloped edge (1675), and two alms-dishes (1686).

On the south side is Warwick Lane, on the west side of which is *CUTLERS' HALL*. The Cutlers have occupied the site only since 1887

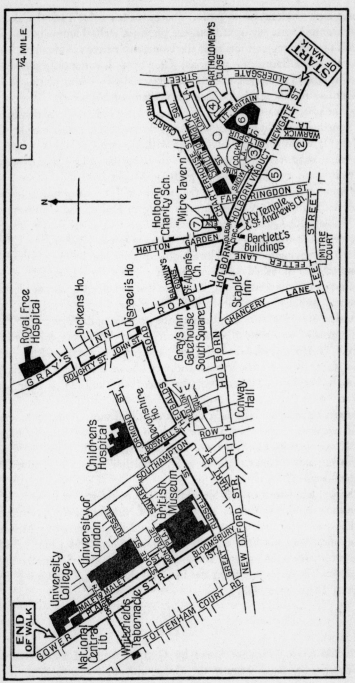

WALK 3. NEWGATE STREET TO TOTTENHAM COURT ROAD. 1. *Christ Church. 2. Cutlers' Hall. 3. St. Sepulchre's Church. 4. St. Bartholomew-the-Great Church. 5. Figure marking end of Great Fire. 6. St. Bartholomew's Hospital. 7. St. Etheldreda's (R.C.) Church.*

previously they were in Cloak Lane. The new Hall is in 'Tudor' style.

Many treasures were brought from the previous Hall. There was an oak panel with an early representation of the Company's crest (an elephant, and on its back a castle flying two pennons) dated 1569; it is the only relic that survived the Great Fire. There was also old armorial glass—some dating from 1674. There were late seventeenth-century chairs of Master and Wardens. Amongst the plate was a silver-gilt loving cup (1616); a salt-cellar in the shape of the Company's crest, profusely jewelled—the cup being on the elephant's back—(1658); a two-handled silver cup with the arms of the Company (1689). There were stained glass windows showing the processes of the cutler's craft, in memory of Francis George Boot, Master in 1894-5.

There were paintings as follows: the widow of John Craythorne—who bequeathed the Belle Sauvage Estate on Ludgate Hill to the Company— (1569); William III; Queen Anne; a traditional portrait of Henry IV. There were water-colour drawings of the Belle Sauvage Inn and Yard.

The Hall was severely damaged by a high-explosive bomb. The north wall was completely demolished, and a large part of the floor was destroyed, as also was the court drawing-room. Other rooms remained undamaged and it has been possible to continue to hold Court meetings at the Hall. The frieze outside, showing various phases of the craft, is undamaged.

The Company lost three eighteenth-century punch bowls, but the charters of Henry V (1416), Queen Elizabeth (1560) and James I (1607), and the portraits and plate, including the items mentioned above, have been preserved. There has also survived a Master's ivory hammer (1603) and an iron poor box in the form of an elephant and castle.

On the same side as the Hall, near the corner of Newgate Street, there was, up to the outbreak of the blitz, a stone with an effigy in low relief of Guy, Earl of Warwick, with the date 1668. This has disappeared.

At the west end of Newgate Street is St. Sepulchre's Church (c. 1670). It has escaped damage.

The thoroughfare west of it is Snow Hill. The police station here, which stands on the site of 'The Saracen's Head' Inn, of *Nicholas Nickleby*, remains, but the Dickens Memorial, a few yards away, which was erected by Messrs. Ormiston and Glass, has been entirely destroyed. There was a bust of the novelist, and terra cotta panels showing the departure of Squeers and Nicholas Nickleby by coach from the Inn, and the flogging of Squeers by the latter at Dotheboys Hall.

SMITHFIELD

is approached from Newgate Street by Giltspur Street. London's most ancient church, St. Bartholomew the Great, the choir of which in part dates from about 1130, has escaped with slight damage.

The gap north of St. Sepulchre's Church represents the site of a parish watch-house erected in 1791. Whilst the church was saved, the watch-house was entirely destroyed.

The figure of a boy at the corner of Cock Lane, erected to commemorate the stopping of the Great Fire at this point (it is said once to have had an inscription, but this has disappeared) was removed for safety. Nicely re-gilded, the boy was restored to his old position in the early part of 1946.

On the east side of Smithfield is

ST. BARTHOLOMEW'S HOSPITAL. It was founded by Rahere at about the same time as the church (1123). The Hospital was entirely rebuilt in 1730-60 and again, for the most part, in 1904-7.

During the War a great deal of superficial damage was done to almost all the buildings but the only serious damage was to the clinical lecture theatre, to the Clerk's house (forming part of the Great Hall block, which is scheduled as an ancient monument) and the old Gibbs' west wing. In addition, super-ficial damage was done by near misses to two of the ward blocks. The Church of St. Bartholomew's Hospital (the parish church of St. Bartholomew-the-Less) escaped except for broken windows resulting from blast.

The statue of Henry VIII (1702) over the Hospital Gate remains.

In May 1946 the 400th anniversary of the Hospital re-foundation by that monarch was specially commemorated.

In Bartholomew Close is

BUTCHERS' HALL. The Butchers have been here only since 1885. Pre-vious Halls were appropriately in the parish of St. Nicholas Shambles (east end of Newgate Street), and in the neighbourhood of Eastcheap. The present Hall, wainscoted in light oak and enlarged in 1913, was damaged in a Zep-pelin raid in September 1915; all the stained glass windows were destroyed including one to Shakespeare (1877) and another to Defoe (1883). The Com-pany, until the Hall was reinstated in 1916, met at the Guildhall.

In the recent War it was again damaged, first by blast in 1941, then by flying bombs in July 1944. Of nine of the new stained glass windows, only three have survived—one dedicated to the Peace of 1919, another to Shake-speare and a third to Wolsey. The fathers of both of these men are said to have been butchers. Amongst the windows destroyed was the second in memory of Daniel Defoe (c. 1920); he was certainly the son of a butcher, and was himself admitted a liveryman, as shown by the following entry in one of the Company's books: 'At a Court held in Pudding Lane, Daniel Foe, son of James Foe, citizen and butcher of Fore-street, Cripplegate, attended to apply for his admission by patrimony and was admitted accordingly, and paid in discharge of serving all offices, £10. 15s. 0d.

The Company saved its plate which included a silver goblet (1669), and a Beadle's staff (1718). Also saved was the Master's chair, presented in 1890. It was made of wood taken from the pens of old Smithfield Market.

The doorway remains, surmounted by the Company's arms and motto: *Omnia subjecisti sub pedibus oves et boves* (He has put all things under his feet, all sheep and oxen. Psalm 8).

'John Carpenter' in the *Evening News*, 4th March 1946, said:

The Worshipful Company of Butchers, one of the great City Companies, are planning to build a new Butchers' Hall to replace the one that stood in Bartholomew-close until it was blitzed.

They want £250,000 to do it; and they are going to ask the meat-producing countries of the world to contribute.

Mr. J. B. Swain, the Master of the Butchers' Company, is to be their envoy. He is to leave London in May for a good-will tour of South America, Australia, and New Zealand. 'I expect to be away for nine months,' he tells me.

He showed me a leather-bound book that he will take with him. It contains messages to the overseas meat traders from the Lord Mayor of London, Sir John Anderson, and the Duke of Norfolk.

This week-end Mr. Swain left on a motor tour of England and Scotland to obtain signatures of the Lord Mayors and municipal chiefs of twenty-two cities.

To enable Mr. Swain to complete his mission he is to be made Master of the Company for the second year—something without precedent in its records.

The New Zealand Meat Producers' Board have contributed a sum of £1,000 towards the cost of the new Hall.

Running north from Smithfield Market is Charterhouse Square. Here is *CHARTERHOUSE*. The name is taken from Chartreuse in France, where the Carthusian Order commenced in 1084. Some part of the early fifteenth-century priory buildings remains. The Guesten Hall (early sixteenth century) was improved (c. 1564) by the Fourth Duke of Norfolk who was executed in 1572. From his time also dated the fine staircase. The chapel of Charterhouse was the Priory Chapel, much restored.

The roof of the beautiful Guesten Hall was burnt off. The panelling had been removed, and the fireplace (c. 1613), though somewhat damaged, remains. 'The ancient chapel', wrote a *Times* correspondent, 'had a remarkable escape. The fire crept along a running beam from the burnt-out cloisters almost into the interior of the chapel, which was saved by cutting down the staircase and by the resistance of its great oak door.' The vestibule of the chapel has sustained damage; the tablets in memory of Leech and Thackeray (both scholars here) have gone, but the one to Wesley is intact.

The Master's lodge, the Registrar's house, the Brothers' library and the Wray library (the more valuable books had been removed), the tapestry room, with its splendid ceiling built by the Duke of Norfolk (the tapestries had been removed), the museum, and music rooms are all shells. The fine

Elizabethan staircase is damaged. The Doctor's house (eighteenth century) and the gatehouse escaped.

The Hall, formerly occupied by the Merchant Taylors' School after the Charterhouse School went to Godalming, was gutted by fire.

HOLBORN

Returning to the main thoroughfare of Holborn by Charterhouse Street, on its west side we find Ely Place. Here is

ST. ETHELDREDA'S (R.C.) CHURCH. It dates from the latter part of the thirteenth century and is all that remains of the London palace of the Bishop of Ely. There was restoration from time to time, particularly in 1874, when the Roman Catholics recovered it from the Welsh Episcopalians, who had used it badly. On 23rd June 1874 the first mass was celebrated, and it is the only building now used for Roman Catholic worship which was so used in medieval times.

It has a large east window, filled with stained glass at the expense of the Duke of Norfolk. The west window commemorating Catholic martyrs had, after long delay, been completed shortly before war broke out. The church is a fine specimen of Decorated Gothic architecture and the south-west doorway is treasured by students of architecture. The wooden screen is modern (1899); it is the work of J. F. Bentley, the architect of Westminster Cathedral.

The church has suffered slightly from bombing. The west window has been broken. The lights illustrating the English Catholic martyrs (Sir Thomas More and Bishop Fisher) and the Carthusians have holes through them, but the recent glass illustrating the life of Father Lockhart (under whose auspieces the Chapel returned to the ancient worship) is intact. The Royal Arms of Charles I, placed in the vestibule by the Catholics (they had formerly been over the communion table) and a holy water stoup found beneath the crypt and believed to date from Romano-British times, are intact.

Mitre Court, on the west side of Ely Place (therein is a modern tavern with an old mitre sign on its façade) leads to Hatton Garden. On the east side is the *HOLBORN CHARITY SCHOOL* designed by Wren in 1696. It has been badly damaged. The figures of a boy and girl on the façade had been removed, as also had the tablet commemorating celebrated residents, erected at the instigation of the present writer's late friend, E. Kilburn Scott, A.M.I.C.E., M.I.E.E. The medallion of Mazzini (commemorating his residence at No. 5 in 1837) remains.

Close by, in Charterhouse Street, a First Folio of Shakespeare (1623) was destroyed by bombing. It had been taken there by a diamond merchant to be placed in a case and sent to South Africa.

Returning to Holborn, to the east is

HOLBORN VIADUCT, bridging the steep descent from Holborn Hill to Skinner Street. It was opened by Queen Victoria in 1869. It has not been damaged in the blitz but two of the statues have gone—Sir Hugh Myddleton and Sir William Walworth, on the north side. The two on the south side—Sir Henry Fitz-Ailwin (London's first Mayor) and Sir Thomas Gresham—remain. The bronze statues representing Commerce, Agriculture, Science and Fine Arts, are not damaged.

West of the Viaduct is the

CITY TEMPLE. It was erected in 1874 for the ministry of Dr. Joseph Parker. John Summerson oddly says it was 'consecrated' and adds, 'It was basilican in form and Italian in character, evincing that lack of sensitiveness which is so invariable in Victorian nonconformist architecture as to seem deliberate.' The piers and galleries were of cast iron, so most of them stood up to the bombing. The pulpit of Caen marble was the gift of the City Corporation. It has now entirely gone and the church is a ruin. The portico is intact and a bust of Parker has survived. The congregation met for more than three years at the Church of St. Sepulchre, Newgate. In June 1946 it removed to The Friends' Meeting House, Euston Road.

Next to the City Temple is

ST. ANDREW'S CHURCH. This was a Wren church; it escaped the Great Fire but was rebuilt in 1686. The tower belongs to the previous building but in 1704 it was refaced with Portland stone. It had a richly fretted roof, a fine altar-piece, and an east window filled with good stained glass in 1718. There was a window at the east end of the north gallery bearing the date 1687. The pulpit was of finely carved oak; the lectern was perhaps the finest in any City church. Round the south wall of the church, on the wainscoting, were particulars of some of the benefactors of the parish. One mentioned was:

Isaac Duckett 1620 directed that £400 should be paid to Dr. Gregory Duckett, sometime the parson of St. Andrew, the profit thereof to be distributed to such poor maid servants as do well and honestly serve and demean themselves.

Annually posters are exhibited inviting applications. As there is so little residential property in the neighbourhood, they are probably few.

The church was burnt out on the night of 16th and 17th April 1941. The pulpit, the font, the altar-piece, and all the stained glass windows left in the church were destroyed. One—a three-panel window at the west end—had been removed. This showed: I.The Adoration of the Shepherds. II.The Nativity. III.The Adoration of the Magi. The last was unique, inasmuch as it showed one of the magi as a black man. The glass was by Heaton Butler and Bayne of Covent Garden (1872).

The Registers, from 1556 (Burial) and 1558 (Baptism), were removed from the burning building together with the plate, including the following: two silver-gilt alms dishes, the centre engraved with the sacred monogram

The hall of the Barbers' Company, built by Inigo Jones, perhaps the most beautiful room to be seen in any of the Livery Companies' premises, which was completely destroyed. Holbein's picture of Henry VIII granting a charter to the Company was saved

Below. *All that remains of St. Andrew's Church, Holborn, illustrated above. It had a richly-fretted roof, a well-carved pulpit, and the finest lectern of any City church*

The memorial to Constance Whitney in St. Giles's Church, Cripplegate, which was damaged (left). The grid-iron weather vane which fell from the spire of St. Lawrence Jewry when the church was destroyed. Below. A bastion of the Roman wall, near St. Giles's Church, uncovered by bombing

*The ruins of Christ Church, Newgate, which was built by Wren in 1687
and (below) those of St. Olave, Hart Street, in which Samuel Pepys and
his wife were buried*

of the cross, the edge inscribed in Greek, and underneath each dish the date 1724; a silver-gilt chalice, with embossed wreathing round lip and base and on the side pricked St. Andrew's Cross with letters 'S.A. Holborn' and above 'S.A. 1624'; a silver gilt cover or paten inscribed 'The Gift of the Lady Elizabeth Richardson widdow, An. Dom. 1635'; two copper-gilt flagons, with St. Andrew and his cross engraved on the sides; two copper-gilt chalices engraved with the figure of St. Andrew and his cross (1799); a small silver chalice with engraved figure of St. Andrew and his cross, and hall-marked George III; a small silver-gilt tray (George III period); two Beadle's staves, with silver heads crowned with mitres, embossed with figures of St. Andrew and his cross and inscribed 1783; a large brass salver, with embossed design of Adam and Eve, serpent and Tree of Life in the centre (date unknown; it was possibly of Flemish workmanship).

The tower of the church remains. Also, on the outside of the north wall is a 'Resurrection' stone, representing the Last Judgment. This probably dates from about the period of the erection of the church. It was originally over the entrance to the pauper burial ground in Shoe Lane, wherein the body of Thomas Chatterton was interred (1770). Two similar carvings remain in London—at the churches of St. Giles-in-the-Fields and St. Stephen, Coleman Street (see p. 49).

BARTLETT'S BUILDINGS. These are on the south side, out of Holborn Circus. Here was the oldest name-plate in the City inscribed

BARTLETTS BVILDINGS
1685

Unfortunately the tablet was broken in demolishing the building upon which it stood. (In Devereux Court, Strand, on the Grecian Restaurant, there is a bust of the Earl of Essex, who died in 1646, and beneath it is inscribed, 'This is Devereux Court, 1676.' This is in the City of Westminster.)

At No. 335, High Holborn is

STAPLE INN. The Hall dated from 1581; the chambers were probably late seventeenth century. The garden was laid out by the Prudential Assurance Company who bought the property in 1886.

Nathaniel Hawthorne's 'little island of quiet' was invaded in September 1944. The Hall was destroyed by a flying bomb. Most of the surrounding chambers were wiped out. A modern pump—its date is 1937—remains; also the Tudor houses, very much restored.

On the other side of the Road (at No. 22) is

GRAY'S INN. The Hall dated from 1556-60. It was a fine specimen of Tudor architecture. It had a magnificent oak screen, a minstrels' gallery with carved front, and windows emblazoned with armorial glass. There was a bench table and a real cupboard.

The Hall had a narrow escape from an incendiary bomb in the first European War. Alas, in the second, whilst the panelling was saved, the Hall was reduced to a shell, as also was the adjoining chapel. Most of the latter was much more modern than the Hall. There was considerable restoration in 1893, when a new roof was constructed.

The library was gutted by fire and about 32,000 books were destroyed. Amongst these were Brian Walton's Polyglot Bible (1657); the 'Treacle' Bible; and complete collections of old English and Ecclesiastical laws of the sixteenth and seventeenth centuries. Amongst the books saved are: Raleigh's *History of the World* (1614), Erasmus's *Novum Testamentum* (1518), Littleton's *Tenures* (1588), and Guicciardini's *Historiae Italicae* (1566).

The statue of Francis Bacon, unveiled by Arthur Balfour in 1912, was removed after the pedestal was damaged. It has now been brought back and is recumbent against the south wall of the hall. The only damage is a small hole in Bacon's right shin.

The chambers in which Dickens worked as a boy—in the office of Ellis and Blackmore, 1 South Square—have been rather badly hit. The Holborn Gatehouse has been damaged and rendered unsafe.

The Gardens are undamaged. The fine wrought-iron gateway remains, bearing the date 1722. So does the catalpa tree (bowed nearly to the ground), erroneously said to have been planted by Bacon, in which belief slips from it have been transferred to America. It can best be seen from Theobald's Road.

Retracing steps a few yards brings the walker to Gray's Inn Road. On its east side are Baldwin's Gardens. Here are the ruins of

ST. ALBAN'S CHURCH. It was erected in 1863; the architect was William Butterfield. It had a lofty chancel arch, in front of which was the great rood, suspended by chains according to Continental ideas. There was a fine triptych exhibiting, in six compartments, incidents in the martyrdom and translation of St. Alban, and in the wings, eight large figures of English saints, and twelve smaller ones. At the west end there were two lofty windows of three lights: this was the most impressive part of the church. There were two chapels. In one was a cross made from the plank on which was laid the body of Father Mackonochie whose first chapel (1862) was a room over a fish-shop in Baldwin's Gardens. In 1887 he was found dead in Memore Forest, Ballachulish (Scotland) and carried on a plank to Kinloch. In the other chapel was the cenotaph, with a lifelike effigy of St. Alban's first vicar, whose body rests at Woking. It was on his death that Mrs. Hamilton King wrote:

> Down in dim St. Alban's
>   The seven lamps burn aglow,
> And softly in the sanctuary
>   The priest moves to and fro;
> And with one heart the people pray,
>   And this is home below.

From 1887 to 1913 when he died, the famous Father Stanton was vicar here.

The church was badly burnt and the stonework much damaged but, says Mr. John Summerson: 'In the ruin there is still everything of the forceful eccentric spirit of its architect.' The Stanton chantry chapel has sustained less damage than the rest of the building. Plans for the rebuilding have been drawn by the brothers Sir Giles Gilbert Scott and Mr. Adrian Scott, architects for the rebuilding of the House of Commons.

Farther north in Gray's Inn Road is the

ROYAL FREE HOSPITAL. It was founded in 1828 but the present buildings were erected between 1897 and 1916.

It was damaged in October 1940, July 1944, and February 1945. There were many casualties in the second 'incident'; in the third, a rocket caused severe damage to the medical school.

THEOBALD'S ROAD

Theobald's Road is east of the British Museum, and is approached by Hart Street. No. 22, where Benjamin Disraeli was born (1804), remains. It has been somewhat damaged and the L.C.C. plaque is missing.

Opposite are the gardens of Gray's Inn (see p. 79).

John Street (north side) leads to Doughty Street where, on the east side is the Dickens House. It was not damaged and was reopened on 22nd June 1946 by Mr. H. C. Dickens, O.B.E., grandson of the novelist and president of The Dickens Fellowship, almost exactly twenty-one years after the opening by the Earl of Birkenhead. The exhibits had been stored for safety in the vaults of Barnard Castle Town Hall. Two new exhibits are 'The Empty Chair', which figured in Sir Luke Fildes's famous picture and 'The Little Wooden Midshipman' (see p. 99).

The last turning but one on the north side, from the east end, is Boswell Street. The L.C.C. regrettably changed the name from Devonshire Street, although Johnson's friend had no local association. It had been called Devonshire Street after Devonshire House, which was on the west side and was erected in 1667 by Lord Cavendish, who became third Earl of Devonshire. In 1934 Major Benton Fletcher purchased the house and presented it to the National Trust, together with old musical instruments and period furniture and pictures. The house was entirely destroyed in the blitz. Major Fletcher died on 31st December 1944. He had expressed a wish that any compensation paid should be used by the National Trust to purchase the house where he died (3 Cheyne Walk, Chelsea).

The baker's shop on the corner stands in remarkable isolation in so devastated an area.

Approached by Boswell Street is

GREAT ORMOND STREET CHILDREN'S HOSPITAL. It was founded in 1852 and received some assistance from Charles Dickens. A new Out Patients' Department was added in 1908. It was attacked in September and October 1940, in January 1941 and lastly in March 1944, when fire broke out.

South of Theobald's Road at this point is Red Lion Square. Here, Conway Hall, the home of rationalism, survived but the Gothic *CHURCH OF ST. JOHN* has been badly damaged. It was built in 1874-8 and is considered J. L. Pearson's masterpiece. The stone vaulting was worthy of the best achievements of the Middle Ages. Pearson's drawings exist and the church may some day again be seen in its old beauty.

BLOOMSBURY

From Theobald's Road, Great Russell Street is reached by crossing Southampton Row. Here is *THE BRITISH MUSEUM.* It was damaged by six high-explosive bombs that fell in the autumn of 1940; remarkable to relate, two failed to explode and thus reduced the damage that otherwise must have resulted. Great structural damage was caused on 16th November 1940, when a high-explosive bomb fell in the Pediment Hall at the north end of the new Parthenon Gallery, recently built at the cost of the late Lord Duveen from the plans of the late John Russell Pope of New York and not yet opened to the public. The whole of the elaborate glass roof of the gallery was destroyed.

The chief damage was done on the nights of 10th and 11th May 1941. Ten of the upper galleries of the Museum were destroyed, including the Greek Bronze room, one of the Greek Vase rooms, the room of Greek and Roman life, the Prehistoric Saloon, the Roman Britain room, the Coin and Medal room, and the roof of the main staircase. Happily the exhibits had been evacuated from the galleries to safe quarters, except a few objects too heavy for removal. On the same night the south-west quadrant of the Museum's main book-stack was burnt. About 150,000 books were destroyed. They were mostly works on medicine, law, archaeology, and the arts, published within the past hundred years or so, and it is believed that none were irreplaceable.

On 20th October 1940 there was a direct hit on the Newspaper Repository at Colindale. 'Here', wrote *The Times* correspondent, 'the scene after the bomb was one of indescribable confusion, with mangled newspaper files piled high and even draping the surrounding roofs. Some 30,000 volumes of bound newspapers were destroyed, mostly English provincial journals of the nineteenth century, but including also some eighteenth-century files. This was a loss which it may never be possible to replace entirely.'

The names round the dome of the Reading room—Chaucer, Caxton,

Tindale, Spenser, Shakespeare, Bacon, Milton, Locke, Addison, Swift, Pope, Gibbon, Wordsworth, Scott, Byron, Carlyle, Macaulay, Tennyson, Browning—were placed there in 1907. They have not disappeared as the result of enemy action; they were expunged during redecoration in the spring of 1939.

The Reading Room was vacated in October 1940 and the North Library was used until June 1946, when the readers were again under the dome.

In April 1946 a small exhibition was opened to the public in the Edward the Seventh Galleries.

North-east of the British Museum is Malet Street. Here is the
UNIVERSITY OF LONDON. In September and November 1940 four high-explosive bombs fell on this fine modern building which had been taken over by the Ministry of Information. There was damage to various parts of the structure and particularly to the University library. First-aid repairs were carried out.

In the adjacent Malet Place is the
NATIONAL CENTRAL LIBRARY. This was presented by the Carnegie United Kingdom Trust and opened by King George V in 1933. The more important bibliographical records, including catalogues containing three million entries, had been removed when the building was badly damaged on 17th April 1941. On that night 110,000 books were lost. The west wing was temporarily roofed at the second-floor level.

West of Malet Street is Gower Street. Here is
UNIVERSITY COLLEGE. It was erected in 1828. The architect was William Wilkins.

It has been most unfortunate. In September 1940 the Great Hall was totally destroyed by a high-explosive bomb. The mathematics department was seriously damaged and subsequently demolished. There was also damage to the library, physics department and gymnasium. In October 1940 an incendiary bomb burnt out two upper floors, comprising the general library, the science library and the Slade School studios. The losses in books amounted to 70,000 volumes, but the rare books had been removed. Amongst those that were lost were books on Scandinavian languages, German language and literature, mathematics, physics, and engineering. In November 1940 the engineering block was seriously damaged. In May 1941 another high-explosive bomb entirely destroyed the applied mathematics department and caused further serious damage to the physics department.

A bust of Sir Thomas Browne was destroyed, but the skeleton of Jeremy Bentham, who died in 1832 and, attired in his own clothes, was kept in a cabinet in the library, had been evacuated for safety to Stanstead Bury (Herts).

The Durning Lawrence Library for students of Shakespeare and Bacon has not been damaged.

West of the British Museum is

TOTTENHAM COURT ROAD

At the north end on the west side was

WHITEFIELDS TABERNACLE. This rather ornate red-brick building was erected in 1903 on the site of a chapel built for the Rev. George White-field in 1756. The large basement hall was named after Toplady, the hymn-writer, as he lies buried beneath it. It was famous for the ministry of the Rev. C. Silvester Horne, M.P.

On 25th March 1945 almost the last rocket to fall on London entirely destroyed the building. Seven people were killed.

Walk 4

Victoria Embankment ★ *Upper Thames Street* ★ *Lower Thames Street* ★ *Tower of London* ★ *The Minories and Aldgate* ★ *Whitechapel*

VICTORIA EMBANKMENT

THE Gothic building at the east end, west of John Carpenter Street, is *SION COLLEGE*. Its foundation dates back to 1630; it was, in its inception, a guild for London clergy, with almshouses. To this a library was added by Dr. John Simpson, rector of St. Olave's Church, Hart Street.

The present building, designed by (Sir) Arthur Blomfield, was erected in 1886. It has suffered through the blitz. The top of the building, on the east side, was bombed away; about 6,000 books were destroyed and many more were damaged. The really valuable ones had been sent away. Included in these were a copy of the first book of Caxton printed in England—the *Recuyell of the Historyes of Troye* (1474)—and a fifteenth-century copy of four of the *Canterbury Tales*. There were other incunabula.

There is a stained glass window in the south wall. It includes figures of St. Augustine, St. Olave, Caxton, St. Martin, Bishop Mellitus, Archbishop Laud, Shakespeare, Chaucer, Edmund Spenser, and Thomas White, the founder. The window has been damaged and only the figure of Caxton is intact.

The lower part of the building is now occupied by the City Livery Club. When they were bombed out of the Chapter House of St. Paul's Cathedral they went to Butchers' Hall. Bombs followed them there, and in December 1944 they again moved—to Sion College.

On the east side of John Carpenter Street is the *CITY OF LONDON SCHOOL*. From Milk Street, Cheapside, the school came to this site in 1882. There has been little damage to the building. The stained glass window in the school hall, with figures of Shakespeare, Milton and Spenser and the statues of Shakespeare, Bacon, Milton, and Newton on the façade are intact.

On the south side of Blackfriars Bridge is Blackfriars Road. Here on the west side was *CHRIST CHURCH*, which was built in 1738-41. It was a plain quadrangular brick building. There was a new chancel erected in 1870. The church has been gutted.

On the south side of it, in Collingwood Street, are some old wooden houses. Farther on (east side) was

THE RING. It was built as Surrey Chapel in 1783 for an eccentric preacher, the Rev. Rowland Hill. Its design excluded corners, where the Devil might lurk. An opening was made for the latter, long after the preacher's death, by the transformation of the chapel into a place of amusement when its use for religious purposes ceased in 1881. From 1910 it was used for professional boxing, and in 1928 Edward, Prince of Wales, was a spectator, with the late Harry Preston of Brighton.

The Ring received a knockout blow from Hitler. There is now only a site to remember it by (north of the existing Surrey Chapel).

On the east side of Blackfriars Bridge is

UPPER THAMES STREET

On the south side, opposite the Church of St. Benet, Paul's Wharf, which is undamaged, is the

WHITE LION TAVERN. Here, on every Saturday in the year, except those preceding Bank Holidays, The Ancient Society of Cogers (founded in 1755) has its debates on the events of the week. Proceedings commence at 7 p.m. and, on the first Saturday in the month, ladies are admitted. The Chair of the Grand Coger is said to be as old as the society. It has sustained some damage in the blitz. It was in Cannon Tavern in Cannon Street at that time, which was the meeting-place when the War started.

Opposite Nos. 26 and 27 there is the churchyard of St. Peter's, Paul's Wharf. The church was not rebuilt after the Great Fire. On the west side is a tablet recording a visit to the church by John Evelyn in 1649.

A few yards farther on at No. 199 is Little Trinity Lane. Here was the PAINTER-STAINERS' HALL. The Company has been on the site since the sixteenth century. The last Hall was built in 1670, the previous one having been damaged in the Great Fire. Extensive repairs were carried out in 1776-7. A new wing was built in 1880. At one time there was a ceiling ornamented by allegorical paintings by Isaac Fuller of Pallas, or the Triumph of the Arts. This was removed about a hundred years ago.

There are a number of portraits: Charles II; William III by Kneller, presented by the artist; the portrait of a queen, probably Mary, William's Consort; Queen Anne; William Camden, in his dress as Clarencieux—presented to the Company by the Master in 1676. Camden left £16 to the Painter-Stainers for the purchase of a cup upon which was put, in accordance with his instructions, an appropriate inscription (1623). There are several

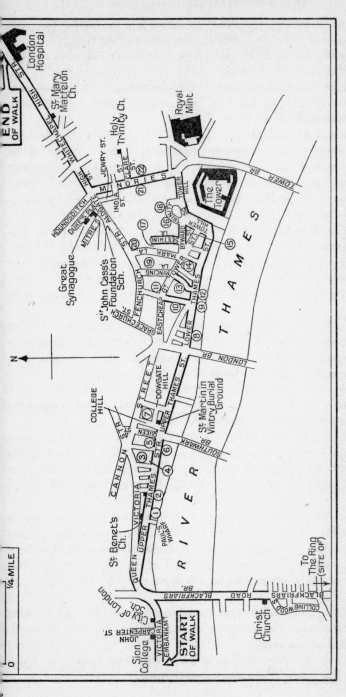

WALK 4. VICTORIA EMBANKMENT TO WHITECHAPEL. 1. *White Lion Tavern.* 2. *St. Peter's Churchyard.* 3. *Painter–Stainers' Hall.* 4. *Tower of St. Mary Somerset.* 6. *St. James Garlickhithe Church.* 6. *Vintners' Hall.* 7. *St. Michael Paternoster Royal Church, Innholders' Hall, Dyers' Hall, Skinners' Hall, Tallow Chandlers' Hall.* 8. *St. Magnus the Martyr Church.* 9. *Billingsgate.* 10. *Watermen's and Lightermen's Hall.* 11. *St. Margaret Pattens' Church.* 12. *Customs House.* 13. *St. Dunstan's-in-the-East Church.* 14. *Bakers' Hall.* 15. *All Hallows' (Barking) Church.* 16. *Port of London Authority.* 17. *St. Olave's Church.* 18. *Trinity House.* 19. *Clothworkers' Hall.* 20. *Tower of All Hallows' (Staining) Church.* 21. *Inmie, Laurie, Norie, and Wilson.* 22. *Sir John Cass Technical Institute.*

other seventeenth-century cups and some tankards of the same period. All the portraits and plate have survived the destruction of the Hall.

A little distance east there are fine views of St. Paul's Cathedral and the ruined churches of St. Nicholas Cole Abbey, and St. Mary-le-Bow.

Farther on, on the same side, is the tower of the church of St. Mary Somerset. The rest of the building was demolished in 1872.

A short distance ahead on the north side is

ST. JAMES GARLICKHITHE CHURCH. There was a church on the site in 1170. Either this, or its successor, was burnt in the Great Fire. Wren designed the previous church, which was completed in 1683. It has two side aisles, separated from the nave by Ionic columns, elevated on lofty bases encased in wood. The walls are panelled in oak to the height of nine feet.

It suffered some damage at the west end but of less serious character than many other churches. A bomb fell through the roof but did not explode. The medieval mummy, kept in a wooden case in the vestibule, came through unharmed. The plate and registers (the latter commence from 1535) have also been preserved. The clock, with a quaint gilded figure of St. James, which was suspended over Garlick Hill, was destroyed. The tower had to be repaired.

On the south side of Upper Thames Street is

VINTNERS' HALL. It is one of the very few of the Companies' Halls undamaged. The swan carved at the entrance is a reminder that the Vintners share with the Dyers' Company the charge of the King's cygnets.

After passing the approach to Southwark Bridge, on the left is the disused burial ground of St. Martin Vintry, a church not rebuilt after the Great Fire.

A short distance ahead on the north side is

ST. MICHAEL, PATERNOSTER ROYAL CHURCH. There was a church here in the early part of the thirteenth century. About 1409 there was rebuilding. The second church was burnt in the Great Fire. The third was completed in 1694 by Edward Strong, Wren's master-mason, under his direction.

The interior is not remarkable. There is a fine oak altar-piece, above which is a picture of Mary Magdalen anointing the feet of Christ, by William Hilton. It was presented in 1820 by the directors of the British Institution. There is a well-carved pulpit, and the ceiling is coved at the sides. Amongst four memorial windows was one to Richard Whittington, who was buried in the pre-Fire church.

A bomb caused the roof to crash, the interior was wrecked and the windows were destroyed. The seventeenth-century fittings had been removed. The tower and walls survived.

The following are extracts from a letter from Canon Douglas which appeared in *The Sunday Times* (6th October 1946):

The other day the man engaged in reconditioning it (the Church) came upon an almost perfect mummified cat, which seemingly had been sealed up in the cavity behind a cornice under its tower.

The probability is that the poor beast was accidentally trapped. But there is also a possibility that following the old pagan tradition of dedicating a building with a human or other living sacrifice, Wren's builders bricked it in as suitable and symbolic for Whittington's rebuilt Shrine. In any case the find is suggestive and interesting, and the authorities of St. Michael's propose to preserve it as a museum piece.

In College Street, south of the church, was

INNHOLDERS' HALL. The Company has been on the site since Stow's *Survey of London* was published (1598) and it may have been there long before. The old Hall was rebuilt after the Great Fire (c. 1670). This Hall was replaced in 1886. It was a handsome panelled room, with the arms of the Company prominently displayed. The Company owned some valuable plate: a salt, made in 1614 and presented by Anne Sweete in memory of her husband in 1635; the Thomas Hinde cup (1654); the Nicholas Cooke cup (1654); the Thomas Charlett tankard (1656); the Edward Osborne cup (1658); the William Pennington tankard (1661) and the Stockton cup (1682).

There is a grandfather clock bearing the Company's arms (c. 1679), and a small clock encased in wood from a beam of the old Hall; a stained glass window showing a cavalier taking a stirrup cup from 'mine host' at an inn door; and a cistern dated 1685.

An illustration in the history of the Company, published in 1922, is of the finely carved front door, 'showing on wall the marks left by German bombs'. Alas, in 1941, they left more than marks—there was serious damage. Happily all the above-mentioned treasures were saved.

In May 1946, the Prime Minister, the Rt. Hon. C. R. Attlee, attended at the Hall to receive the Freedom of the Company. His family had been connected with it through the firm of Druces and Attlee, Solicitors, who had been clerks to the Company for nearly 250 years.

A little farther on is Dowgate Hill. Here, on the west side, are:

1. *DYERS' HALL.* The site was acquired in 1657. The present Hall and offices date from 1840-56, but there was some seventeenth-century stained glass. The hall, reception rooms, and offices sustained damage in the blitz, but the ancient fittings, furniture, charters, and portraits were saved and also a curious muniment chest, probably of Flemish manufacture, a warden's mahogany chair (1730), a barge master's badge (1746), and a barge master's crook for catching swans (the Dyers' and Vintners' Companies have the responsibility of making two nicks on the king's cygnets on the River Thames).

2. *SKINNERS' HALL.* The present Hall is on or near the site of the first one (thirteenth century). It dates from 1668-9, having been rebuilt after the Great Fire. A new front was added in 1791: it is Ionic in character, with the Company's arms on the pediment. The fittings and decorations were com-

pletely altered in 1847-8. There is a fine old staircase. The hall has survived, but the old oak parlour and Clerk's room were entirely destroyed. and damage was caused to panelling in the beautiful cedar drawing-room. The Company's plate has survived. This includes five silver-gilt loving cups in the form of cocks, of which the heads must be removed for the purpose of drinking (1605). They were bequeathed by William Cokayne. There is a snuff box in the form of a leopard, the dexter supporter of the Company's arms. Another treasure is a fine funeral pall.

3. *TALLOW CHANDLERS' HALL*. It has been on the site since 1476. The Hall, rebuilt after the Great Fire by Wren and completed in 1672, was extensively altered in 1881. It had a decorated ceiling, and panelling and mirrors to a height of thirty feet. The court room on the second floor is wainscoted to the ceiling, which was gilt. The carving of the entrance door dates from 1894.

The south wall was damaged and in part destroyed by a high-explosive bomb. First-aid repairs were executed and, despite further loss of stained glass through a flying bomb, it was made usable and has been the meeting-place of some twenty other Companies.

All the treasures have been saved. These include a grant of arms and crest (1456); a book of accounts from 1550 in the original binding; an early seventeenth-century oak table; a tall case clock of walnut (c. 1700).

There is a fine wrought-iron gate left. This bears the Company's arms and its motto *Ecce Agnus qui tollit Peccata Mundi* (Behold the Lamb of God which beareth the sins of the world).

On the east side of the arch is All Hallows Lane. Here is a belfry which belonged to All Hallows the Great Church and took the place of the tower which was demolished in 1876, as was the church in 1893. A short distance ahead on the right will be seen a board bearing the inscription 'Hour Glass Tavern'. The latter has entirely disappeared through bombing. It had a watch house attached and this bore a foolish inscription stating that it had been erected in 1557. The actual date was 1807. A few yards ahead is the church-yard of All Hallows the Less; the church was not rebuilt after the Great Fire. Through the bombing there has disappeared a tombstone, with an inscription in Welsh commemorating Owen Jones and his son of the same name. The father was a great collector of Welsh literature. After his death his collection was bought and presented to the British Museum. The son was an architect who superintended the building and decoration of the Great Exhibition in Hyde Park in 1851.

LOWER THAMES STREET

On the east side of London Bridge is
ST. MAGNUS THE MARTYR CHURCH. There was a church here

at the time of the Norman Conquest. Wren rebuilt it, as a result of the Great Fire, in 1676. The steeple was added in 1705. It is divided into a nave and side aisles by slender Ionic columns. The ceiling is arched and ornamented with fretwork. There is a handsome altar-piece with Corinthian columns.

The church sustained damage by blast on five occasions but it has not been of a serious character. The woodwork was either sent to the country or placed in the strong room. None of the treasures has been lost. These include what is said to be a piece of the Holy Cross 'duly authenticated'; relics of a number of saints; a Russian icon; a pre-Reformation paten (c. 1500); a large 'basson for the ewse of the Porre' (1524); a cup (c. 1590)—said to be the parcel-gilt goblet referred to by Mistress Quickly in Part 2 of *Henry IV*, Act II, Sc. 1); a copy of Murillo's picture *St. John the Baptist*; and a figure of St. Magnus. There is also a tobacco box from the church of St. Michael, Crooked Lane (demolished in 1831 in consequence of the erection of the new London Bridge) and, from its graveyard, the tombstone of Robert Preston, drawer at the Boar's Head Tavern, who died in 1730. It has the following interesting inscription:

> *Bacchus, to give the toping world surprise*
> *Produced one Sober Son, and here he lies.*
> *Tho' nurs'd among full Hogsheads, he defied*
> *The charms of Wine, and ev'ry vice beside.*
> *O Reader, if to Justice thou'rt inclin'd,*
> *Keep Honest Preston daily in thy mind.*
> *He drew good Wine, took care to fill his Pots*
> *Had sundry virtues that outweigh'd his faults.*
> *You that on Bacchus have the like dependence,*
> *Pray copy Bob in Measure and Attendance.*

The stone is in a yard behind the church.

The clock that hangs from the tower (it was removed for safety during the blitz) was the gift of Sir Charles Duncombe in 1709, the year in which he became Lord Mayor.

Opposite Billingsgate Fish Market is St. Mary-at-Hill. Here, on the west side, is the

WATERMEN'S AND LIGHTERMEN'S HALL. The present site was purchased in 1776: before that the Hall was in or near Upper Thames Street. Removal to the new Hall took place in 1780. It has a neat pilastered façade, with a pediment and an ornamental fanlight over the three-light window on the first floor. The hall mantelpiece is of marble, with a figure 'of the God Thames', above which are the arms of the Company. There is a wood carving of the Royal Stuart arms from the old Hall and a portrait of J. Taylor, the 'water poet'. It represents him as being of a fair complexion, with a short beard; his dress, a falling ruff and slashed doublet. H. G. Aldis (*Cambridge History of English Literature*) thought a more correct description of Taylor was 'literary bargee'. Amongst the Company's treasures is a loving cup (1695) and a barometer surmounted by the arms of the Company (1695). The Watermen and Lightermen are not a Livery Company.

On looking up St. Mary-at-Hill, there is a fine view of the spire of St. Margaret Pattens' Church, Eastcheap; it is 200 ft. in height. The church is one of Wren's (1687).

Further on, on the south side is the

CUSTOMS HOUSE (near London Bridge). This is the fifth on the site, all the four previous ones having been destroyed by fire. There has been damage through bombing, but not of a serious character.

On the other side of the road is St. Dunstan's Hill. Here is

ST. DUNSTAN'S-IN-THE-EAST CHURCH. There was a church on the site in 1100. As Stow (1598) described it as ancient, it may not have been rebuilt up to his time. In 1633 there were extensive repairs. In 1666 it was burnt in the Great Fire.

Wren rebuilt the church about 1671. The fine steeple was not completed until 1699. It is considered Wren's finest work of this kind. There are four arched ribs which support the lantern and spire, the latter terminating in a ball and vane. The total altitude to the summit of the vane is 180 ft. 4 in. It is seen to the best advantage from the foot of St. Dunstan's Hill or from the centre of London Bridge. Wren, in rebuilding the church, used much of the old material, and by 1810 the fabric had become greatly decayed and the walls were found to be forced as much as seven inches out of the perpendicular by the pressure of the roof of the nave. As reparation was considered to be impossible, the church was pulled down, except the steeple, and a new church, designed by David Laing, was erected between 1817 and 1821. It was Perpendicular Gothic in style; it had two side aisles, divided from the central portion by slender clustered columns and pointed arches, above which was the clerestory. From the capitals of the columns rose single shafts to meet the roof of the nave, which was decorated with graceful fan tracery.

The church was badly damaged in September 1940. The clerestory walls were demolished. The spire remains. On 2nd October 1946, the ceremony of beating the parish bounds was revived.

At No. 17 Lower Thames Street is Harp Lane. On its east side was

BAKERS' HALL. From 1506 the Bakers had a Hall here. The last had been erected in 1719-22, after its predecessor had been destroyed by fire.

It was restored by James Elmes about 1825. It had a good oak screen, with Corinthian columns and pilasters, a mantelpiece of Queen Anne detail with pink Verona marble (1932), and a handsome old basket grate and fireback. Over the fireplace there were six large barge shields of Elizabethan tapestry portraying the Company's arms. They were for the decoration of the Company's barge at the time when the Lord Mayor's pageant was held partly on the river. There was a Flemish candelabrum and a lacquered clock made by Thomas Gardner, a member of the Clockmakers' Company, in 1689. The carved doorway and overdoor of the court room had been taken from the Earl of Chesterfield's mansion at Holme Tracey.

The Hall has been destroyed. The Master's chair and the Company's banner have gone. There have survived the clock, the barge shields, the charters (1486 and 1569) and the plate. Amongst the latter are a gilt wine cup (1606), a porringer (1670), a tankard (1681), and a barge master's badge of the same period.

It is proposed to re-erect the Hall on the old site and to the same plan as the one destroyed.

A little farther ahead, on the left, there is a good view of the ruined Church of All Hallows Barking and, behind, the huge building of the Port of London Authority.

At the east end of Lower Thames Street is the

TOWER OF LONDON

Attributed to Julius Caesar by Shakespeare and, more surprisingly, by Thomas Gray, the Tower was actually erected on the initiative of William the Conqueror. The great keep, known as the White Tower, was commenced about 1078. There were many towers added in the medieval period and other intermittent additions were made up to the eighteenth century.

During the air attacks on London the Tower received fifteen direct hits from high-explosive bombs. Three flying bombs dropped within its walls and innumerable incendiaries, but no vital damage was done. One bomb dropped near the White Tower and exposed a subterranean tunnel. The medieval buildings were not seriously affected but considerable damage was done to the Tudor buildings and to their glass.

In the King's House, built by Henry VIII, in which Anne Boleyn is said to have spent her last night and where, seventy years later, Guy Fawkes was examined, Hess was lodged for three days and nights. On 15th August 1941 Josef Jakobs, a spy, was shot on the miniature rifle range.

Two of the casualties of the blitz were the famous ravens. One of the staff relates that, before the War, he was showing a Nazi official round and drew his attention to these birds. 'Oh,' said the German, 'in our country we have eagles.' 'One of the ravens must have heard him,' said the guide, 'for it immediately bit him.' The Tower has now only one raven—'Grip', aged 16. 'Mabel', aged 14, mysteriously disappeared in 1946. It is believed to have been kidnapped.

It is estimated that 75 to 80 per cent of the American troops who came to this country visited the Tower. It was reopened to the general public at the beginning of 1946.

On 21st May 1946 there was revived the custom, dating from 1923, of placing lilies and roses in the Wakefield Tower on the spot where it is believed Henry VI was murdered (1471). This is done at the expense of Eton College, of which he was the founder.

In Byward Street, west of the Tower of London, is
ALL HALLOWS' BARKING CHURCH. The somewhat misleading name of this church is derived from Barking (Essex). In the seventh century the Abbey was granted rights over land upon which the first church was built, probably about 675. The name now preferred is All Hallows-by-the-Tower.

It offered remarkable architectural features. The earliest parts were the nave arcades, which dated from about the middle of the thirteenth century. Possibly the lower part of the east wall was of the same date. In the middle of the fifteenth century the chancel arcade, and the chapels at the east end, were rebuilt. The east window, of five trefoils, was of fourteenth-century date.

The north porch and the room over it were built in 1883 at the expense of Canon Mason, who was then vicar. The figures are St. Ethelburga, Virgin and Child, and Lancelot Andrewes. There are also displayed the arms of Barking Abbey and of the Diocese of London.

The tower was erected in 1659—the only surviving feature of a City church which dated from Commonwealth times. Pepys ascended it to watch the progress of the Great Fire of London. He wrote in his diary under the date of 5th September 1666: 'I up to the top of Barking steeple and there saw the saddest sight of desolation that I ever saw.'

That sight was nearly equalled in 1941 when the church was reduced to a shell. The tower remains, as also does the north porch.

The fourteenth-century crypt is intact. It includes a chapel dedicated to St. Francis of Assisi (c. 1350). There is also a model of Roman London, and a tablet commemorating the place where the body of Archbishop Laud lay from the time of his execution on Tower Hill, in 1645, to the time of his re-interment at St. John's College, Oxford, in 1663.

The church was the richest in brasses of any in the City. There were fifteen in all, the earliest being that of William Tonge (1389). They were all covered with asbestos mats and it is hoped that they are none the worse for the bombing. It was the church of Toc H. The first 'lamp of maintenance', given by the Prince of Wales, as patron, in 1922 in memory of friends of whom the War bereft him, has survived, as also has the casket which enclosed it. There has also been preserved the figure of Alfred Forster, son of Lord Forster of

Fragments of a great Saxon Cross, which once stood on Tower Hill. They fell out of the bomb-shattered walls of All Hallows by the Tower, where they had been for at least 800 years

The beautiful font of All Hallows by the Tower was destroyed with the church, but the richly-carved cover had been taken to St. Paul's Cathedral

Tubs of flowers in the ruins of All Hallows by the Tower mark the sites of the great pillars. Still standing is the tower from which Pepys watched the Great Fire

Above. *Presenting the prize for the pancake 'greaze' in the ruins of West-minster School.* Below. *The damaged roof of Westminster Hall reflected in the pool of water left by the fire-fighters' hoses on 10th May 1941*

Above. *The four towers of St. John's, Westminster, on account of which the church has been likened to an upturned footstool. Below. Chelsea Old Church, one of London's most unhappy losses*

Lepe, to whom Australia owes the beginning of Toc H in the Commonwealth. The Purbeck marble tomb of John Croke (who died in 1477) has survived; the monument to the daughters of Sir Peter Colleton, the work of Peter Scheemakers, has been badly damaged. The font was destroyed but the cover was preserved by removal to St. Paul's Cathedral. There is now a new bowl. It has been made out of limestone from Gibraltar, and was presented by tunnellers in memory of their comrades who lost their lives in rendering the Rock impregnable. The pulpit (1613), reredos (1685), altar table (1636), and chancel screen, the gift of the Hanseatic League (1705), have all been destroyed.

One of the last additions was a stained glass window at the east end of the south aisle, presented by the Port of London Authority. It showed the City, with old London Bridge. This has been destroyed.

Here, William Penn, founder of Pennsylvania, was baptized (1644). The memorial tablet, erected by the Pennsylvanian Society in 1911, has been badly damaged, and the inscription is only partly legible.

As a result of the blitz, there were two most interesting discoveries at All Hallows' Church.

Behind the organ, which had occupied the west end of the church, and concealed by panelling, an arch was found. It is formed of Roman tiles without a keystone, and is believed to date from the latter part of the seventh century.

The other discovery is thus described by the Rev. P. B. Clayton:

Out of the wall adjacent to the arch great fragments fell, which had for at least 800 years been embedded as the capstones in the strong Norman pillars of that date. Some of these stones were most remarkable. The Keeper of the Medieval Department of the British Museum announced them to be unparalleled. . . . The pillar has preserved them to this age intact, unique, alone, and unexampled. They represent a school of craftsmanship whereof we have no other evidence. They form a portion of a noble Cross which once upreared its head on Tower Hill, before the Norman William conquered London.

Pictures of the fragments are reproduced in this book. On 1., T. D. Kenrick, Secretary of the Society of Antiquaries, says: 'Two warriors with short cloaks, their legs cross-gartered, are "resolutely English" in design.' On No. 2, 'Two naked legs with ankles bound suggests a London martyr, who fell a victim to the heathen Danes. The lettering suggests the name of Earconworth.' There seem to be two animals in fierce combat. In this respect there is similarity with the Danish memorial stone found in St. Paul's Churchyard (see p. 55). The cross at All Hallows' Church is believed to date from about 1030.

Opposite All Hallows' Church is Seething Lane. Here is the ruined *ST. OLAVE'S CHURCH*. It was built in the middle of the fifteenth century, but there is a crypt of the early thirteenth century. It was small and a good example of the Perpendicular style of architecture. It had a north and south aisle, separated from the central portion by clustered columns of Purbeck marble and pointed arches, over which was a clerestory with small windows. It was restored in the reign of Charles I, about 1632; there were further alterations in 1731-2 and in 1870-1, when the galleries were removed.

The church has always been pre-eminently associated with the diarist, Samuel Pepys. In 1669, his wife was buried here. She was only twenty-nine. Her husband erected a handsome memorial, with bust, in the chancel. It is believed to have been designed by John Bushnell. There was a long Latin inscription which said she bore no children for none could be worthy of her. Samuel Pepys was buried in the same church in 1703, but there was no memorial until 1884 when, on the site of the Navy gallery, James Russell Lowell unveiled a tablet with medallion.

The church has been reduced to a shell but happily both the Pepys memorials had been removed. Also, the finely carved pulpit (it came from the Church of St. Benet, Gracechurch Street) had been preserved in the crypt of St. Paul's Cathedral.

Among the interesting monuments that have been destroyed are the following:

Sir John Radcliffe, son of the first Earl of Sussex (1568); Anne Radcliffe, second and divorced wife of the second Earl of Sussex (1585); Sir James Deane (1608). The last was shown with three wives. One was facing him as he knelt—presumably the last; one of the other two turned her back to her spouse. Below were shown chrisom children lying on their backs. The chrisom cloth, shown on their heads, was worn for a few days after christening, and this indicated that they died when a few days old. Mistress Quickly said of Falstaff that he 'made a finer end and went away an it had been any christom child', and Bunyan says of Mr. Badman that he 'died like a Chrisom-child, quietly and without fear'. This was the only instance of chrisom children on a London monument. There were also monuments to Andrew Bayning (1610); Paul Bayninge, a sheriff in 1593 (1616); Em. Charlton (1622)—her monument displayed three skulls and an hour-glass; Sir John Mennes (1671), as Comptroller of the Navy he figures much in Pepys's Diary; and Sir Andrew Riccard (1672). The last was chairman of the East India Company and of the Turkey Company.

The church has some interest for Americans by reason of one of sixteen monuments brought from the Church of All Hallows Staining, when that church was demolished in 1870. This showed a reclining figure of Commerce with weeping infants. It was erected to Monkhouse Davison and Abraham Newman. They are said to have supplied part of the tea which was sent to Boston, U.S.A., and there thrown into the harbour.

The tower of the church stands. On its wall is a tablet recording the miraculous preservation of the daughter of the Rev. J. Letts, who (c. 1840) fell from the top floor of the rectory on to the paving stones in the basement.

The gateway in Seething Lane also remains. It bears three stone skulls, two of which are impaled on a spike. Of this Dickens wrote in his essay *The City Churchyards* (1860). To him, it was the church of 'St. Ghastly Grim'. There is a Latin inscription *Christus Vivere More* (If Christ lives death is gain to me), followed by part of a date—16. . . .

The church possesses valuable plate: late sixteenth-century cups; a flagon of 1607; a paten of 1612; a dish of 1691; a flagon of 1692. There is also a large dish with gadrooned edge and the royal arms, and letters C.R. This was of late seventeenth-century date and came from the Church of All Hallows Staining. All the above have survived.

In Trinity Square, north-west of the Tower of London, is

TRINITY HOUSE. This building, designed by Samuel Wyatt in 1793-5, has been seriously damaged. It had a fine façade with Graeco-Roman details, and some well-decorated rooms. Most of the contents, including ships' models, have been destroyed. The outside walls can be repaired and plans have been prepared for the reconstruction of the interior.

Close by, in a garden, is the scene of public executions. The removal of the railings has made the spot, which is marked by a tablet, accessible to the public. The last to be executed by axe was the Scotch Lord Lovat (1747). Through the collapse of a stand, about twenty people lost their lives when waiting to witness the death of a man who was in his eightieth year.

On Tower Hill, at the north-east corner of the Tower of London, is

THE MINT. It was designed by John Johnson, Surveyor of the County of Essex, and completed by Sir Robert Smirke. The east side and façade have been damaged by bombing.

West of the Tower of London is

GREAT TOWER STREET. No. 34, which was the finest specimen of an old business house left in the City, has been entirely destroyed. It had a flight of stone steps with a balustrade. The courtyard in which it stood has also disappeared. It had been in occupation by Dent, Urwick and Yeatman, Wine Merchants, for many years. (There is an essay on the house in W. G. Bell's *Unknown London*.)

North of Great Tower Street is Mincing Lane. Here was the

CLOTHWORKERS' HALL. The Company has had its Hall on this site since the middle of the fifteenth century. The last Hall was erected in 1856-60 and was opened by the Prince Consort. It had a front of Portland stone, with Corinthian pilasters. There were five stained glass windows showing the arms of the Company and its past masters and benefactors.

The Hall was destroyed on the night of 10th May 1941. The Company lost all its furniture, a carved gilt figure of a ram, from the state barge (late seventeenth century), two wooden figures of James I and Charles I (saved from the Great Fire), three windows containing late seventeenth-century heraldic glass, and the library. The strong room escaped injury and the plate was saved, together with one hundred boxes of charters and title-deeds, minute-books from 1520, some china and portraits. Amongst the plate were two rosewater dishes (1605 and 1616); college cups (1657); a loving cup (c. 1660); a gilt ewer and dish, tankard, and salt-cellar (1676); a ewer and rosewater dish (the gift of Samuel Pepys, Master, 1677); a salt-cellar, and flagon (1680); a tankard (1683); and a gilt salver (1684).

Close by, at the north end of Mark Lane, is the fifteenth-century tower of All Hallows' Staining Church. It has stood alone since 1870, when the rest of the building was demolished. In the churchyard is a crypt of Norman architecture (c. 1156) from Lamb's Chapel, Monkwell Street. It is said to have been one of the buildings of the Hermitage of St. James's-on-the-Wall. It was bequeathed to the Clothworkers' Company and, in 1873, removed to its present position. It is now open to the public.

THE MINORIES AND ALDGATE

The Minories run north from the Tower of London to Aldgate High Street. On the east side is St. Clare Street. Here was

HOLY TRINITY CHURCH. It had been used as a parish room since 1899, when the parish was united with that of St. Botolph, Aldgate. It was of much interest. A gravestone on the floor, consisting of a slab of marble, recorded the death, in 1596, of Constantia Lucy, daughter of Thomas Lucy, Junr. This was a grand-daughter of Sir Thomas Lucy, once supposed to be the original of Mr. Justice Shallow, and Shakespeare's *bête noire*. There was a monument on the north wall to Colonel William Legge who died in 1670. He married Elizabeth Washington, niece of Lawrence Washington, the great-great-grandfather of George Washington. The Washington arms were shown—the stars and stripes—impaled upon Colonel Legge's escutcheon. Another monument was to Lord Dartmouth who died in 1691.

Here also, in 1852, was found in the vaults the mummified head supposed by some to have been that of the Duke of Suffolk, father of Lady Jane Grey, who was beheaded on Tower Hill in 1554. This was removed to the Church of St. Botolph in 1899.

The building has been entirely destroyed and all its monuments. There can still be seen, close to where was the entrance (it is near to a G.P.O. inspection cover), a small square stone inscribed '1745'. Beneath was deposited a box filled with bones brought from the field of Culloden.

The north wall, stripped of plaster by blast, shows traces of window and other openings formerly belonging to the north wall of the chapel of the nuns of St. Clare. A seventeenth-century font has gone to the Church of St. Lawrence Jewry (see p. 58).

No. 123 Minories (west side) was the shop of Imrie, Laurie, Norie and Wilson, Chart Publishers. Inside, was the 'little wooden midshipman' of *Dombey and Son.* The shop has been badly damaged but happily in 1940 the midshipman had been evacuated to St. Ives (see p. 81).

Crossing Aldgate at the north end of the Minories, Mitre Street is reached. On the right is the shop of J. E. Sly and Son, Dealer in Sacks, Ropes, etc. It is said to date from 1650, and, remarkably, it has survived.

Opposite is the Sir John Cass Technical Institute.

In Duke's Place, opposite Jewry Street is

SIR JOHN CASS'S FOUNDATION SCHOOL. Founded in 1710 in Aldgate, on the corner of Houndsditch, it was removed to the present site in 1869. The south wing of the school was demolished by a high-explosive bomb. The science room in the north wing was burnt out. On the outbreak of war the 250 scholars had been evacuated to Aylesbury. In Holy Trinity Church there they celebrated, each year, the Founder's Day, but went to a cinema as a substitute for the usual dinner. In February 1946 Founder's Day was again celebrated at the Church of St. Botolph, Aldgate, when some two hundred children attended. They wore red quills, in accordance with the old custom commemorating a legend that Sir John Cass, whilst in the act of signing his will, burst a blood vessel and stained the quill he was using.

Also in Duke's Place is the

GREAT SYNAGOGUE. The site has been occupied since 1722. The Synagogue was rebuilt in 1790. It has been entirely destroyed, and all the treasures were lost, including a fine eighteenth-century painting of Moses and Aaron.

WHITECHAPEL

East of Aldgate is Whitechapel High Street. Here, on the south side is *ST. MARY MATFELON CHURCH.* Probably there has been a church here since the early part of the fourteenth century. It was rebuilt twice at least. The present building dates from 1882. It has been gutted by fire.

Farther east, in Whitechapel Road, is the

LONDON HOSPITAL. England's largest hospital (it has about 900 beds) was founded in 1740, in Prescott Street, Whitechapel. In 1760 the building on the present site commenced. There has been alteration and addition, and in 1876 a new wing was added.

It has suffered much from enemy action.

On 8th September 1940 the first raid did considerable damage to the nurses' homes and the laundry. There were no casualties but the Hospital was left without gas or water. The next day all patients were removed t Chase Farm, Enfield.

On 20th September 1940 another bomb fell but caused little damage. O 23rd September 1940 (the bi-centenary of the Hospital), it was visited by th King and Queen. The following night a bomb fell in the main garden bu did not explode. After many attempts by the bomb disposal squad to mov it, it was blown up by the famous Lieutenant Davies, after having bee covered with five hundred sandbags. No damage was caused and Lieutenan Davies was presented with the stethoscope he had borrowed with which t listen to the ticking of the bomb.

During October 1940, incendiary bombs were of regular occurrence. O 10th October the roof of one of the nurses' homes was fired. It took eight fire engines two hours to extinguish the flames. On 21st October, during dinner three bombs arrived without warning. Two hit the colleges, badly damagin; the laboratories and the anatomical department. On 8th December 194 a fire was again caused in one of the nurses' homes.

On 16th March 1941 over forty incendiary bombs were at one time aligh on the Hospital, but the only severe damage was to the carpenters' shop. O 10th May 1941, the night of the last heavy raid on London, there were ove two hundred casualties. There was then a long period of immunity.

On 17th June 1944, there was some damage from a flying bomb. On 3r August 1944 the Hospital received the worst blow of all. The following i an account from *The London Hospital Illustrated*, 1945:

When the newspapers recorded in August 1944, that some hospitals had been hit b flying bombs, no names were mentioned. But one of those was the 'London'.

It happened in the early hours of the morning. Had it been day-time the casualtie would have been heavy, but, as it was, only two patients were killed, two nurse injured, and there were some minor casualties. But that, again, is tragedy enough The bomb landed, fair and square, on the middle of the East Wing, where the kitche of the Nurses' Home is on the top floor. The heavy equipment crashed through th five floors into the Steward's Stores in the basement.

It wrecked Royal, Wellington, Mary and Cambridge Wards.

Royal and Wellington Wards were named in 1842 respectively after the then Princes Royal and the Great Duke, a Vice-President; Mary was named after the then Duches of Gloucester in 1773; and Cambridge was named after the first Duke of Cambridg in 1835.

The whole Hospital was badly blasted, particularly the old Nurses' Home in th East Wing, the Nurses' and Maids' Dining Rooms, the Steward's Department, an the Pathological Department, while the Paulin covered way across the Quadrangl was badly smashed by blocks of flying masonry.

Rescue squads, who with the police, fire, ambulance, and other Civil Defence Ser vices, were quickly on the scene, were much hampered by water, of which more tha 300,000 gallons cascaded down from the smashed water-tanks on the roof.

Later, the electric light failed, but the Hospital's emergency lighting quickly cam into use providing 1,500 lights. The Sisters came on duty in their wards immediately

Patients in the damaged wards and children were moved temporarily to other wards. Only one emergency operating theatre was found fit for use, but it was in action at once.

In spite of the dislocation caused by the damage to the Steward's Department, one thousand four hundred meals of cereals, eggs and bacon, and marmalade were served at breakfast-time, much to the satisfaction of patients, doctors, nurses, students, lay and domestic staffs and Civil Defence helpers. This was made possible by taking over the kitchens of the Medical College and the Doctors' Mess.

During the day the evacuation took place of all the patients who could be moved. Large motor-ambulances took them, together with nurses, to the Annexe at Brentwood, Warley Woods Hospital, and other hospitals in the sector controlled by the London'. Maternity cases were taken to the Hospital's own maternity homes in Hertfordshire. Children were taken to the Northern Hospital of the London County Council.

By the evening, thanks to the marvellous work of 'all hands' at the Hospital, and of the Civil Defence workers, 263 beds were ready for patients. This number had risen by the end of the week to 360 beds. No mean feat in the dislocated circumstances.

The damage to the structure of the Hospital was very heavy. The cost is estimated at not less than £100,000. Many hundreds of windows were smashed—frames as well as glass—and scores of doors wrecked. There was also a very considerable loss of stores.

A sequel to the incident was a letter from the firemen paying tribute to the coolness of the Hospital personnel, and to the meal of bacon and eggs. They underlined their tribute with a cheque for £5.

The last 'incident' in the East End was close to the London Hospital. This was on 27th March 1945 in Vallance Road, Bethnal Green. It was the worst with which the Hospital had to deal in five and a half years.

During the War it treated nearly 30,000 patients of whom more than 3,000 were war casualties.

In the same period, Dr. William Smart, head of the Department of Pharmacology, started a small herbal garden. In it have been grown rosemary, rhubarb, fennel, carroway, peppermint; all used in flavouring medicines. There are also belladonna, aconite, and opium poppies. They are not actually used for the purposes of the hospital but for the education of medical students,

Walk 5

London Wall ★ Bishopsgate ★ Shoreditch ★ Clerkenwell

LONDON WALL

FROM the north end of Wood Street, Cheapside there can be reached *ST. ALPHAGE CHURCH* (west of Aldermanbury). Only the porch, which was erected in 1914 in the fourteenth-century style of architecture, remains, but the destruction is not due to bombing. The church was demolished in 1923.

The part of the City Wall north of the porch has been damaged by bombs *ALL HALLOWS' CHURCH* (north side near Old Broad Street). The church was rebuilt by George Dance, Senr. (1765-7), on a site that had been occupied for over six centuries. There was much alteration in 1891.

In the blitz there was damage to plaster and glass, and a candelabrum was destroyed.

In Coleman Street (south side, west of Moorgate) is the *ARMOURERS' AND BRAZIERS' HALL*. This was built in 1840-1 and stands on the site occupied by the Company when, in 1453, it received its first charter. Amongst specimens of armour preserved is that of Sir Henry Lee, Queen Elizabeth's Champion. He founded, and was first President of the Society of Knights Tilters. He retired in 1590. His suit of armour, which was acquired by the Company in 1767, was made by Jacobe Halder who was master-workman in Greenwich armouries. The Hall sustained slight damage in the blitz. None of its treasures has been lost. These include a silver-gilt cup (1553), a flagon (1567), a cup (1568), a maser (1578), and cups of 1580, 1598, and 1608.

In Throgmorton Avenue, on the south side of London Wall near Finsbury Circus, is all that remains of the *CARPENTERS' HALL*. This Hall was on the site of the first (1428-9). It was modern, having been erected in 1876-80. The oak furnishings of the old Hall, which escaped the Fire of London, were used to decorate the new one. Other survivals of the previous Hall were three mid-sixteenth-century paintings on plaster: the subjects were King Josiah commanding money to be given to the carpenters for the repair of the Temple; Christ in the carpenter' shop; Christ teaching in the synagogue and saying 'Is not thys that carpynter [Son]'. For many years prior to the War these paintings had been on exhibition at the London Museum and so have survived.

A land-mine wrecked the building in May 1941, and the destruction was completed by the explosion of gas mains in London Wall.

All the Company's records (continuous since 1438), charters, ordinances, Tudor carvings, furniture, pictures and plate were saved. Amongst the last are steeple cups and covers (1609, 1611, 1613 and 1628), tankard (1653), goblet (1655), porringer (1664), and goblet (1665). Amongst the furniture that has survived is an octagonal oak table with initials of Master and Wardens (1606), and an oak arm-chair of about the same date. There has also been saved the Master's and Wardens' garlands (1561). The Master's garland

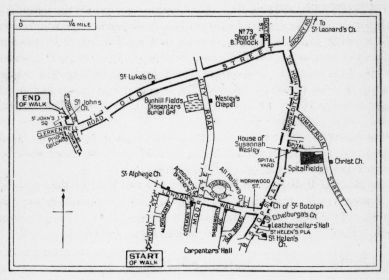

WALK 5. LONDON WALL TO BISHOPSGATE

is of embroidered crimson velvet, set with enamelled silver plaques, bearing the City arms and the Company's arms.

The losses include two Jacobean fireplaces built into the structure of the Hall, and some medieval corbels from the old Hall which could not be removed.

The Company guarded some of the treasures of the Loriners' Company, which has no Hall. Its charters and other documents were found in the safe six months after the fire at Carpenters' Hall (owing to the dangerous condition of the walls, earlier access was impossible). They were found soaked and covered with mildew. Zaehnsdorf (see p. 27) treated them with a solution of benzine and other chemicals, poured from an ordinary garden spray. This killed the mildew. The seals had withstood the damp.

The Company, between 1940 and 1946, trained some thousands of soldiers as carpenters, joiners, timbermen, and whitesmiths at its trade training school in Great Tichfield Street. It is now training demobilized service men, sent by the Ministry of Labour and National Service.

Wormwood Street, a continuation of London Wall, leads to

BISHOPSGATE

The medieval churches of St. Helen and St. Ethelburga are undamaged, as also is the Church of St. Botolph (1729).

In St. Helen's Place, on the east side is

LEATHERSELLERS' HALL. The Company has had the site since 1543, when it acquired the dissolved priory of Benedictine nuns which adjoined the Church of St. Helen. Its premises survived the Great Fire, which left this part of the City untouched, but all remains of the priory were ruthlessly removed in 1799. The present Hall dates from 1878. It has sustained somewhat serious damage but has not been destroyed. The ancient charters (including one of 1444 showing Henry VI in crown and regalia), the muniments, minute-books, library and plate were saved.

BISHOPSGATE INSTITUTE (at No. 230) happily escaped. Here are the Head-quarters of the London and Middlesex Archaeological Society, founded in 1855. It deserves the support of all London-lovers.

At No. 310, Bishopsgate is Spital Square. In Spital Yard, on the south side, is a seventeenth-century house in which was born Susannah Wesley, the mother of the founder of Methodism. It has escaped the blitz but as the free-hold is for sale, it will probably be demolished at an early date.

SHOREDITCH

Straight on from Bishopsgate is Shoreditch High Street. A short distance down Commercial Street, which is on the east side, is

CHRIST CHURCH, SPITALFIELDS. It was designed by Hawks-moor (1729). There is an imposing porch formed by four detached Doric columns. The interior is rectangular, and consists of seven bays with aisles. The western bay has a gallery carried on Corinthian columns, and containing the organ. The pillars bear round arches, above which is a clerestory. It has been badly damaged.

Farther north along Shoreditch High Street is

ST. LEONARD'S CHURCH. It was designed by George Dance the elder (1740). There is a Doric portico and a flight of steps. It has a fine tower, similar to that of St. Mary-le-Bow. At the end of the nineteenth century it was renovated under the direction of Sir Arthur Blomfield. At a later date a rood-beam was added.

On the south wall is a remarkable monument in wood to Elizabeth Benson, who died in 1710 in her ninetieth year. There are shown two vigorous skeleton figures representing Death pulling down the Tree of Life. On the north wall, a grey marble tablet was erected in 1913 in memory of the Elizabethan actors, James, Cuthbert, and Richard Burbage, all buried in the old church. They were associated with London's first theatre, commemorated by a London County Council tablet in Curtain Road, near the junction with Great Eastern Street. Richard Burbage was the first great Shakespearean actor. Also mentioned are Richard Tarlton, Gabriel Spencer (killed by Ben Jonson in a duel) and William Sly.

The church was damaged by a flying bomb in August 1944, but can be restored. Both the Benson monument and the actors' tablet have survived. A stained glass window brought from the demolished Church of St. James, Curtain Road, has been destroyed. It was made in 1886 to commemorate the supposed three-hundredth anniversary of Shakespeare's arrival in London, and illustrated the 'Seven Ages of Man' from *As You Like It*.

In the churchyard there still remain the old stocks and whipping post; also the tombstone inscribed '1807 John Gardner's Last and Best Bedroom'. The stone was erected in the year mentioned by the deceased who survived until 1834. Some time after the end of the war, it was broken in a drunken frolic. It is hoped to piece it together again.

Old Street runs west from the church. Here, on the north side, is Hoxton Street. No. 73 is the Toy Theatre shop which, for many years, was owned by Benjamin Pollock. It was visited by R. L. Stevenson and referred to in his essay *Penny Plain and Twopence Coloured*. Pollock died in 1937, and in July 1944 his daughter sold the stock to Alan Keen, Robert Donat, and Ralph Richardson. They formed a Limited Company (other members are Douglas Millard, a publisher, and Fred Bartlett) under the title of Benjamin Pollock Limited. Then came the flying bombs; they blew in all the windows but happily did little damage to the fabric.

City Road divides Old Street. On the west side of the former thoroughfare, south of the junction, is

BUNHILL FIELDS DISSENTERS' BURIAL GROUND. Bombs have made gaps in the vaults and provided gruesome spectacles. The tombstones of Bunyan, Defoe, Susannah Wesley, Watts, Dr. Williams (founder of a well-known library in Gordon Square), William Blake, etc., have not been damaged.

On the north side of Old Street, some distance west of City Road, is ST. LUKE'S CHURCH. It was built in 1733, the architect being George Dance, senior, and was thoroughly repaired in 1877-8. It is rich in stained glass. It has sometimes been known locally as 'lousy St. Luke's' from a tradition regarding the weather vane. The story goes that the builder, peeved by parsimonious treatment, placed a representation of a louse on the top of the tower. The present writer, after observation with field-glasses, was inclined to accept the story. If louse it was, it has been sacrificed to the war effort—it disappeared when there was a demand for metal. Bombs damaged the roof of the church and destroyed much glass.

CLERKENWELL

A continuation of Old Street is Clerkenwell Road. Here, on the north side is St. John's Square and

ST. JOHN'S CHURCH, CLERKENWELL. The Church of the Priory of St. John of Jerusalem was erected here in 1185; it had then a round nave like the present Temple Church. There was rebuilding after the attack by Wat Tyler rebels in 1381; and further rebuilding by Prior Docwra (1501-27). Much of the church was destroyed by the Duke of Somerset (c. 1548) seeking material for his Strand palace. There was some reparation in the reign of the Catholic Queen Mary. In the early eighteenth century it was used as a Presbyterian meeting-house. In 1723 it was reconstructed as the parish church of St. John. Thus it remained until 1931, when the parish was united with that of St. James's, Clerkenwell, and the church assigned solely for the use of the Order of St. John of Jerusalem.

The church has been badly damaged but the beautiful crypt of Norman and Early English architecture remains. Here is a beautiful effigy of Don Juan Ruyz de Vergara, Proctor of the Langue of Castile in 1575. A child lies to the left of his feet. Here also is the figure of the last Prior—Weston. It was removed from the Church of St. James, Clerkenwell, in 1933.

In St. John's Lane, south of the square, is still the south gateway of the Priory, built by Prior Docwra in 1504.

Walk 6

Westminster Abbey ★ *The Houses of Parliament* ★ *County Hall* ★ *Lambeth Palace* ★ *Tate Gallery* ★ *Victoria Street* ★ *Buckingham Palace*

WESTMINSTER ABBEY

THE damage is of a minor character. The roof of the lantern (Wyatt's work, c. 1820) fell, but fortunately into the central space between the choir and the steps of the sanctuary, where it could do little harm. The pulpit was partly destroyed but there was no serious damage to the fabric or to the monuments. The Chaucer window in Poets' Corner was destroyed. It was installed in 1868, and represented various incidents in the *Canterbury Tales*. There was serious damage to stained glass windows in the chapter-house, and to stonework and glass in Henry VII's chapel. The window in the south-west corner of the nave in memory of George Herbert and William Cowper (1877), the gift of the American, G. W. Childs, has sustained damage. The figure of Herbert has gone, but Cowper remains. There are two brown hares round his feet. In a letter to Mrs. King, dated 25th September 1788, Cowper wrote: 'My two hares died more than two years since; one of them aged ten years, the other eleven years and eleven months.'

The Coronation Chair and the stone embedded beneath the seat (brought to London in 1297 by Edward I; it is believed that all the early Scottish kings were crowned thereon) were removed for safety during the War. The stone was buried near the Abbey, and a plan showing its exact whereabouts sent to Mr. Mackenzie King, the Prime Minister of Canada, in 1940. The plan is being preserved in Canada as an historic relic.

The Deanery of the Abbey has been almost entirely destroyed. The present writer was the possessor of a book not in the Dean's library—a copy of the first Abbey guide in English (1683). He proudly mentioned it to the late Dean (Dr. P. F. D. de Labillière) who died in April 1946. Pride went before a bomb! Alas, he lost it in the following year.

H. V. Morton, writing in *The Times* on 1st May 1946, a few days after the Dean's death, said of the destruction of the Deanery:

A few days later I met him. He was as gentle and as courteous as ever. I have 'nothing except the clothes I stand up in,' he said, as he asked me to go and look at the ruins of the Deanery. Passing through the Jerusalem Chamber, we paused at the edge of a pit that was open to the sky where oak beams were still smouldering, and watched the wind agitating a hideous brittle mass of blackness which had been the Dean's library. 'I think I am the only Dean in history', he said ruefully, as he gazed towards the ruin of his beloved books, 'who has no Bible or Prayer Book.' The only rooms to escape in the whole of the Deanery were two small and never used spare bedrooms.

The Jerusalem Chamber and Jericho Parlour have survived. In the little cloister, three seventeenth-century houses (occupied by Canon Barry, Dr. Bullock the organist, and the precentor, the Rev. C. M. Armitage) and one modern house were burnt out. The library was slightly damaged by an incendiary bomb.

The Jewel Tower (west of the chapter house), which was probably built by Richard II (1377-99), and where at one time the regalia and crown jewels were kept, has sustained some damage.

In Dean's Yard, south-west of the Abbey, is the entrance to *WESTMINSTER SCHOOL*. The large school hall was originally the dormitory of the Benedictine monks of Westminster Abbey. The lower parts of the walls were of late eleventh-century date. It had a hammer-beam roof, dating from the seventeenth century, and below it was the bar over which, on each Shrove Tuesday, the pancake was thrown in accordance with a custom that goes back to the middle of the eighteenth century. The hall has been gutted and so also has Dr. Busby's library, a building erected in the middle of the seventeenth century and possibly designed by Inigo Jones. The dormitory, designed by the Earl of Burlington (1723-30) has been burnt out. The beautiful seventeenth-century Ashburnham House has escaped.

Amongst the débris, wet and dirty, was a photograph of an athletic team of 1937 showing a plump youth whose name was—Ribbentrop. His entry, above the usual age, was permitted as a special courtesy to his father.

Mr. A. L. M. Russell, the School architect, says: 'In the immediate rebuilding and restoration work it is proposed to use brick and not to make any effort to reproduce the style of our old buildings. Our aim is to erect completely new buildings which, although modern, will fit in very reasonably with what remains of the old school.'

He added that the first task would be to rebuild the old dormitory which, only 160 ft. long and 26 ft. wide, had provided accommodation for forty King's Scholars. The King's Scholars, on their return from Bromyard (Herefordshire), where they had been since 1940, occupied the Head Master's house, which was intact.

On 5th March 1946 the pancake 'greaze' was again held. Across the ruined school hall the old beam was fixed up by a rope. The winner this time was presented with (instead of a guinea) a golden sovereign, worth nearly twice as much.

North-east of the Abbey is

ST. MARGARET'S CHURCH. It is a parish church, and the church of the House of Commons. In the main it is a fourteenth-century building, but there has been much alteration from time to time. In 1735 all external ornament disappeared and the tower was almost rebuilt. In 1806 the apse was replaced by a square end. In 1876 there was a restoration which involved the removal of the galleries. Later the east and west porches were added.

The church has not suffered much from bombs. The west window (1882), commemorating Raleigh, whose headless body was buried here (1618), has lost one light. Whilst Queen Elizabeth, Raleigh, Prince Henry, and Edmund

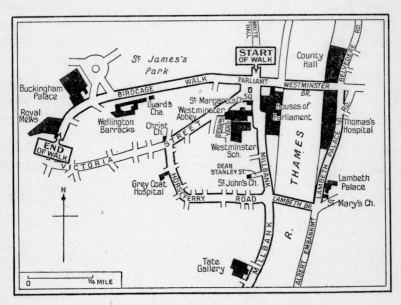

WALK 6. WESTMINSTER ABBEY TO BUCKINGHAM PALACE

Spenser are still shown, Sir Humphrey Gilbert—Raleigh's half-brother—has gone. The Milton window (unveiled by Matthew Arnold in 1888) has also suffered. Here can still be seen Milton at St. Paul's School and in the act of dictating, but the daughters have gone, as also has the glass depicting his visit to Galileo.

The most notable feature of this church is the east window—the finest and most historic in London. It was presented to Henry VII by Ferdinand and Isabella of Spain on the occasion of the marriage of their daughter, Catherine of Aragon, to Henry's eldest son, Prince Arthur. It has been thrice removed for safety; first in the Civil War, when it was in the private chapel of the Abbot of Waltham at New Hall (Essex) and General Monk saved it from destruction; a second time on the outbreak of the War of 1914-18; a third time during the War of 1939-45. It was again reinstalled in the early part of 1946, and looks better than ever; probably because of the cleaning it has undergone.

South of Westminster Abbey and approached from Millbank by Dean Stanley Street is

ST. JOHN'S CHURCH, which dates from 1728. The architect was Thomas Archer. It has a portico supported by Doric columns and a tower at each corner. This is not (as a mythical story goes) due to Queen Anne's turning over a footstool and requesting a church in resemblance; it is owing to the swampy soil on which it stands. The interior was highly ornamented. It has been reduced to a shell.

THE HOUSES OF PARLIAMENT

PALACE OF WESTMINSTER. The oldest part of the Palace of Westminster, the official title of the Houses of Parliament (derived from the King's Palace which was here until about 1530) is Westminster Hall. This was erected by William Rufus between 1097 and 1099. It was then divided by a double row of columns. The Hall was remodelled and heightened by Richard II (1394-8): he removed the columns and erected the magnificent roof of oak. The entrance front was restored in Bath stone in 1819-20.

The Chapel of St. Mary Undercroft was completed in 1327. The cloisters were built between 1526 and 1529. The upper part of them was destroyed by the fire of 1834, in which most of the old palace disappeared. The new building was commenced in 1840 and completed in 1852.

The following are particulars of enemy attacks, taken from an excellent book by Sir Bryan H. Fell, K.C.M.G., C.B., late Principal Clerk in the House of Commons:

On 12th September 1940 an oil bomb struck the West Front and started a fire, which was quickly put out.

On 26th September 1940 a high explosive bomb which fell in Old Palace Yard caused severe damage to the south wall of St. Stephen's Porch, the tracery of the Great Window in this wall, the War Memorial under the window, and the masonry of the West Front.

On 10th May 1941 a deliberate attack appears to have been made on the Houses of Parliament. At least twelve incidents are recorded on this night in various parts of the building, and four people were killed. The Commons Chamber was entirely destroyed by a fire which spread to the Members' Lobby and caused the ceiling to collapse. The roof of Westminster Hall was also set on fire. Part of the lantern and a considerable area of the roof boardings and rafters were destroyed, but the trusses do not appear to have suffered to any great extent. A small bomb or an anti-aircraft shell struck the Clock Tower at the eaves of the metal roof and destroyed some of the ornamental ironwork and damaged the stonework. All the glass in the south clock face was broken,

St. Anne's Church, Soho, before bombing which left only the walls and the tower. Two curious features were the square chambers flanking the sides and the barrel-like construction near the top of the tower, bearing the clock

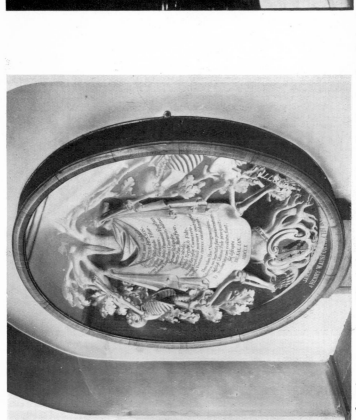

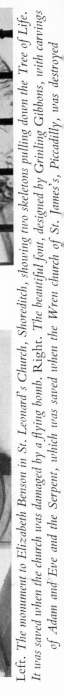

Left. The monument to Elizabeth Benson in St. Leonard's Church, Shoreditch, showing two skeletons pulling down the Tree of Life. It was saved when the church was damaged by a flying bomb. Right. The beautiful font, designed by Grinling Gibbons, with carvings of Adam and Eve and the Serpent, which was saved when the Wren church of St. James's, Piccadilly, was destroyed

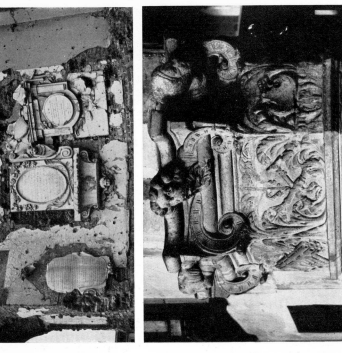

Left. This carving of Ezekiel's Vision, attributed to Grinling Gibbons, was one of the treasures rescued from the badly damaged church of St. Nicholas, Deptford. Above. Some of the damaged memorial tablets on the walls of St. Anne's Church, Soho. Below. One of the capitals ascribed to Holbein in the More Chapel of Chelsea Old Church

Charles I returns to Whitehall. The statue was sent to Lord Rosebery's country home for safety and a strong-point, disguised as an information bureau, built round its plinth in preparation for invasion

but the clock and bells were undamaged and the chimes and hours were broadcast as usual. The House of Lords was struck by a bomb which passed through the floor of the Chamber without exploding. The north side of Peers Court, the Government and Labour Whips' Offices, and a number of other rooms were destroyed.

Capt. E. H. Elliott, Resident Superintendent, was killed at his post while assisting the fire fighters. Two policemen and a custodian were also killed.

On 22nd January 1944, incendiary bombs set fire to the roofs of Westminster Hall and the Grand Committee Rooms without doing serious damage, and on 15th July 1944, a flying-bomb which fell on St. Thomas's Hospital, broke a large number of windows on the Terrace front.

In all there was damage to the Palace of Westminster on seventeen occasions.

None of the mural paintings in the corridors has been destroyed. All the historical treasures, such as the letter from Charles I to the House of Lords, appealing for the reprieve of the Earl of Strafford, the death warrant of Charles I and the manuscript prayer book attached to the Act of Uniformity (1662), were removed for safety. A fine bust of Cromwell, attributed to Bernini but more probably by Ruysdael, was also taken away.

Within a few days of the destruction of its Chamber, the House of Commons sat in Church House, Dean's Yard, and on 21st November 1941 the king opened the new Session in the Hall of Convocation. It was thus occupied for about seventeen weeks in 1940, 1941, and 1944. Appropriately the Rt. Hon. Winston Churchill attended here to receive the Freedom of the City of Westminster in May 1946.

The House of Commons now meets in the Chamber of the House of Lords. The Lords are accommodated in the King's Robing Room, specially fitted up for the purpose.

A new House of Commons is under construction. The architect is Sir Giles Gilbert Scott, O.M., R.A., and the engineer Dr. Oscar Faber, O.B.E., D.C.L. (Hon.), D.Sc. The scheme prepared by these two gentlemen was approved by the Royal Fine Arts Commission, recommended by the Committee and agreed to by the House on 25th January 1945. The cost will be approximately £784,000 on the basis of 1939 prices, and the work is expected to occupy six years.

In March 1946, it was announced that skeletons, believed to be of fifteenth-century date, had been found when excavating in the cloisters. It was decided to hold an inquest.

In Parliament Square, facing Whitehall, there was from 1941-5 a faked bookstall, which was a concrete defence post. This was a strategic device at the time when invasion was possible. It was the work of Capt. Jack Reginald Crowe, a scenic artist of Anerley, who was a Home Guard officer.

COUNTY HALL

is on the south-east corner of Westminster Bridge. The home of the London County Council was erected by stages between 1913 and 1933. The original architect was Ralph Knott, F.R.I.B.A. It contains about a thousand rooms.

County Hall has suffered much damage—from high-explosive bombs, oil-bombs, and blast. The worst damage was caused by a land-mine on the terrace just outside the middle (crescent) portion of the river frontage. The parts affected were mainly the offices; the Council chamber suffered minor damage which did not prevent its continued use. Some committee rooms were rendered useless. The pillars and external wall along the crescent portion of the river frontage will have to be pulled down and rebuilt.

The one ancient relic in County Hall remains. This is a fireplace from 59 Lincoln's Inn Fields, and is in the members' waiting-room. It is believed to date from 1752. A recent acquisition is a bust of Bernard Shaw by Sigmund Strobl. It has been placed in the ambulatory of the council chamber pending the opening of the National Theatre.

It is remarkable that a barbed-wire barricade was across Belvedere Road as late as June 1946. It was not surprising that 'Godsibb' (in *London Town*—organ of the L.C.C. staff) wondered if 'just a few of the very high-ups . . . had not yet heard the news that the War is over'.

At the south-west corner of Westminster Bridge is
ST. THOMAS'S HOSPITAL. It originated in the Priory of St. Mary Overy (where is now Southwark Cathedral), in the early thirteenth century. In 1228 a new hospital was built on the east side of Borough High Street. Here it remained until 1871, when it was transferred to the present site on the Albert Embankment.

It has been the most unfortunate of the London Hospitals in the recent War. The following is a résumé of 'incidents' based on the 'War Diary' kindly lent through the courtesy of the Governors.

9TH SEPTEMBER 1940. At 2.30 a.m. a large bomb struck Block 1 (the Blocks are numbered from Westminster Bridge). It caused the collapse of three floors, and the deaths of two nurses and four masseuses who were crushed in the masonry. The transformer room was buried, and the cable severed; thus the only supply of direct current was cut off, and the lifts were put out of action. The X-ray department also had to cease operation, and the gas supply began to fail. As the water supply ceased completely on 10th September many patients were transferred to Botley's Park and Woking War Hospitals.

13TH SEPTEMBER 1940. Two bombs fell almost simultaneously. They caused another great fall of masonry, and the shattering of nearly every window in

Blocks 7 and 8. There were, however, only a few casualties and only one was serious.

15TH SEPTEMBER 1940. At 8.30 p.m. very heavy bombs made direct hits on the main corridor immediately south of the Central Hall, penetrating to the basement, and causing the collapse of the medical out-patients' Block and the sitting-room of College House, wrecking the kitchen, canteen, dispensary, and administrative Block, and putting all the essential services of the hospital out of action. Two house surgeons and a nurse were killed, and subsequently a woman at a first aid post died from injuries. There were no casualties amongst the patients. As a result of this incident most of those who had not already been evacuated were transferred to Botley's Park and Woking. There were, however, always a few patients, in addition to war casualties, who remained. It was decided to reserve fifty casualty beds in the basement wards of Blocks 2 and 3.

15TH OCTOBER 1940. At 9.10 p.m. heavy bombs struck the Northcote Trust room, blowing up some of the staircase on Block 7, and wrecking City Ward. Except for small cuts, there were no injuries. There was almost incessant bombing throughout the night, and a flow of casualties from two neighbouring shelters which had direct hits. Thirty-two injured persons were admitted to the wards, and eight others were brought in dead. A new ward was made in an old bed store. It was called 'Scutari', owing to its likeness to the rooms (at that place) in which Florence Nightingale nursed the sick; the name is still retained.

8TH DECEMBER 1940. A shower of incendiary bombs fell on and around the buildings. Three serious fires might have followed—one in the timber store adjoining the carpenters' shop, one in the debris of E hut, and one in the ruins of the medical out-patients' department. All three were dealt with quickly and effectively by the Hospital fire-fighters.

29TH DECEMBER 1940. At 6 p.m. a large number of incendiary bombs was dropped on and around the Hospital, while high-explosive bombs which shook the building considerably fell quite near. Five fires were started on the roofs of Mary ward, Unit laboratory, Christian ward, College House, and the Medical School, but they were all quickly extinguished.

16TH APRIL 1941. This was a terrible night at the Hospital, as it was elsewhere. Incendiary bombs fell all over the main building. The carpenters' shop was burnt out. For hours the turret of Block 7 and the adjoining roof burned fiercely. Debris between Blocks 7 and 8 caught fire and burned for two hours. A succession of bombs shook the Hospital continuously, and blast blew in most of the windows at the south end. Heavy bombs fell in the Nightingale Square, wrecking the interiors of Blocks 2 and 3, the Nightingale Home, and the sanitary tower of Block 2, together with the colonnade which joined the two blocks. Blast from the explosions wrecked the two basement wards, Nuffield and Arthur, from which the patients had to be evacuated immediately. Nuffield ward was, in addition, flooded with water from the tanks on the roof, while the ophthalmic ward, which is immediately above it, caught fire and burned for some hours. Yet, despite all this damage, the only casualty was a slight one—a patient in Arthur ward had her face cut by flying glass. At this time the first convoy of patients, twenty in number, was sent to St. Thomas's Hospital, Godalming.

10TH MAY 1941. On this night the Hospital had its most severe raid. The alert was sounded at 11 p.m. and, at intervals of only a few minutes until 5 a.m., sticks of high-explosive bombs and a great number of incendiaries fell in the surrounding district. The main building received three direct hits; Riddell House (the nurses' home and training school at the corner of Lambeth Palace Road and Paris Street, which was erected as a result of a donation of £100,000 from Lady Riddell) was hit twice, and another bomb fell in the garage yard. Incendiaries destroyed the whole of the top floor of Block 4. The roof and top floor of St. Thomas's Home were also damaged by fire, while the garage, with all the cars in it, the timber store and adjoining buildings were burnt out. Two members of the London Fire Brigade lost their lives as a result of the bomb explosion in the garage yard. Remarkable to relate, there were no casualties among the Hospital personnel or patients.

4TH JULY 1944. A flying-bomb exploded in Bishop's Park at the rear of St. Thomas's House and Riddell House. Extensive superficial damage was caused to the Hospital, Riddell House, and St. Thomas's House, but no one was injured.

15TH JULY 1944. At 3.25 p.m. the Hospital received a direct hit from a flying-bomb which struck the theatre in Adelaide ward in Block 2. Serious and extensive damage was caused. Much of Mary ward, the Matron's house, and the Nightingale Home, the whole of the staircase in Block 2, and the corridor between the Matron's house and Block 2 were destroyed. The accountant's, cashier's, and lady almoner's clerks' offices were rendered quite unusable, while the nurses' dining-room, which was being used as a carpenters' shop, suffered a similar fate. Nuffield ward, in the basement, which had been specially reinforced, had twenty-four patients in bed when the bomb fell. Although the ward shook, it took the strain perfectly, and no one was injured. It was thought advisable, however, to close the ward in case of structural collapse, and the physio-therapy department on the ground floor was hurriedly converted into an emergency ward. Before the evening was well advanced all the patients were in their new quarters. The nurses' preliminary school was then evacuated to Edinburgh and the massage school to Manchester.

Thus concluded the heroic story of bravery and endurance in London's second oldest hospital. It is one worthy to be remembered for all time. It has been honoured in high quarters, as the following announcement in *The Times* for 12th April 1941 showed.

The King has given orders for the following appointments and awards:

The George Medal

H. R. B. Norman, B.M., B.Ch., M.R.C.S., L.R.C.P., Resident Assistant Physician, P. B. Maling, Medical Student, and H. E. Frewer, Assistant Clerk of Works, St. Thomas's Hospital, London.

After St. Thomas's Hospital had been hit by a high explosive bomb, it was found that two of the staff were trapped. Mr. Frewer formed a rescue party, and was joined by Dr. Norman and Mr. Maling.

The debris had crashed through the ground floor into the basement. The dispensary stores had been destroyed and the alcohol and acids caught fire. Gas was escaping and masonry was continually falling. Mr. Frewer led the rescue party. Dr. Norman, assisted by Mr. Maling, burrowed into the debris and gave morphia injections. They succeeded in extricating the casualties.

There have survived the two statues of Edward VI. One, of bronze, dates from 1739. The origin and date of the other, which is a stone statue, are unknown. It faces the river, and can be seen from the footpath running between it and the Hospital.

Another statue that has survived is of Sir Robert Clayton (1701), a Lord Mayor who was generous in his bequests to the Hospital. This statue has been attributed to Grinling Gibbons.

Four stone figures of cripples, which were also brought from the Southwark Hospital, are intact.

The Albert Embankment leads to

LAMBETH PALACE

The London Seat of the Archbishops of Canterbury for nearly seven-and-a-half centuries dating, in some parts, from the early thirteenth century, has suffered damage during the recent war. In all, ten high-explosive bombs and a number of incendiary and flying-bombs fell on the premises or in the vicinity. The worst night was the ever memorable Saturday, 10th May 1941. On that occasion there were three simultaneous fires—in Chicheley's, sometimes known as Lollards', Tower; in the library; and in the chapel.

The chapel fared worse than the other buildings. The east end was badly damaged; the west end was soon a ruin. The wooden screen, that dated from the time of Archbishop Laud, and was surmounted by his arms, was smashed to pieces. The copy of the marble tomb of Archbishop Tait (in Canterbury Cathedral) was also destroyed, only the head of the effigy remaining intact. There still survives a tablet in the chancel floor commemorating Archbishop Parker who died in 1575, and one on the wall commemorating the first

Lambeth Conference (1867). The top of Chicheley's Tower was burnt away, but the prison apartment with wood panelling, iron rings, and inscriptions of prisoners, remains. The fine hammer-beam roof of the library has sustained some damage but can be restored. This dates from 1663, when the old dining hall and roof were restored by Archbishop Juxon.

Since 1829 it has housed the Library which, founded by the will of Archbishop Bancroft who died in 1610, contains 44,000 printed volumes and 1,300 volumes of manuscript. Some of the most valuable books and manuscripts were removed before the blitz commenced. About 8,000 were damaged, probably about half that number beyond repair. Amongst those lost are volumes chronicling the councils of the church, others containing the works of the Early Christian Fathers, and some printed by Froben of Basle, a contemporary of Caxton. The catalogue (an interleaved copy of the Bodleian's) survived almost miraculously. Nearly 150 of the spacious bookshelves, dating from 1829, were destroyed by fire. The bookcase which belonged to Archbishop Laud and came from St. John's College, Oxford (where he was buried), is intact. A window in the north-west angle of the hall, in which was assembled much old stained glass, depicting the arms of archbishops, was entirely destroyed. On the night referred to, the late Archbishop Lang, who was greatly concerned about the fate of the burning library, had a narrow escape from severe blast.

All the exhibits in the library, including the Macdurnan Gospels, the first three editions of More's *Utopia* (1516 and 1518), a cookery book of the time of Queen Anne, with a specimen piece of cake made from one of its recipes, had been removed before the blitz started. The shell of Archbishop Laud's tortoise (when it died in 1753 it was said to be 120 years old) has gone. As a result of bombing, a bell dropped from Chicheley's Tower into the chapel. It bears the date 1685.

Morton's Tower (1490) is quite undamaged, except for the windows. The guard-room, where hung portraits of the Archbishops, received slight damage. The portraits are now back at the palace.

Next to the Palace is

ST. MARY'S CHURCH. It has a long history commencing with a reference in Domesday Book. The present edifice is, for the most part, modern. In 1850-2 there was a thorough restoration, amounting almost to rebuilding, but the tower, probably early fifteenth century, was left.

There has been little damage from bombs. All the stained glass has gone, including the Pedlar's window (1703). The monuments are intact: they include Hugh Peyntwyn (1504) and John Mompesson (1524). There is also a tablet in memory of Tunstall, Bishop of Durham (d. 1559), and Thirlby, the only Bishop of Westminster, who died in 1570. The baptistry in memory of Archbishop Benson, who died in 1896, is undamaged. Here also is the flat gravestone of Elias Ashmole, founder of the famous museum at Oxford. He died in 1692.

In the churchyard there remain the tombs of the Tradescants, seventeenth-century antiquaries and gardeners (a road in South Lambeth, on the site of their house, is named after them), and of Captain William Bligh of the ship *Bounty*, who died in 1817.

On the other side of the river, west of Lambeth Bridge is the

TATE GALLERY

It was opened in 1897. It has a Corinthian portico, supporting a figure of Britannia. The galleries are built round a handsome central hall. On ten occasions it sustained some damage—September, October, and December 1940, January, February, March, April, and May 1941, and from flying-bombs in 1944. The greatest harm was done in 1940 when the roofs of the east and west wings were hit. Throughout the War, the only work of art that was damaged was Richard Wilson's *Destruction of the Children of Niobe*, which was brought to London for cleaning.

The Gallery was reopened to the public on 11th April 1946.

By way of Horseferry Road, which is in a direct line with Lambeth Bridge, one can reach

THE GREYCOAT HOSPITAL (approached by Strutton Ground). It was founded in 1698 but was much altered in 1873. It had on its façade the arms of Queen Anne, who granted a charter in 1706, and a clock turret.

Incendiaries fell upon it on 10th May 1941, and burned out the board-room and the school hall. The old roof with its turret clock crashed to the ground. The quaint figures of a boy and girl in niches were not seriously damaged.

Proceeding north to

VICTORIA STREET

on the north side is

CHRIST CHURCH. It was rebuilt in 1843, but retained from the old church a bell of 1639. The church has been gutted. The Rev. R. J. Campbell, once of City Temple fame, was vicar from 1917 to 1921.

Buckingham Gate, a turning to the west, leads to Birdcage Walk. Here is the ruin of the

GUARDS' CHAPEL OF WELLINGTON BARRACKS. It was built in 1839-40 on the model of a Grecian temple. The interior was not considered worthy of the exterior so, in 1877, the chapel was closed and a sum of money realized from the sale of the Guards' Institute was devoted to the purpose of a complete internal reconstruction. The work was put into the hands of G. E. Street, R.A. (the architect of the Royal Courts of Justice); he built an apse at the eastern end and over it a semi-dome. The side walls of the nave were covered with an arcade enclosing panels of marble mosaic. The heads of the arches were filled in with terra-cotta groups in high relief, representing biblical subjects. The chancel screen and pulpit were of white Sicilian marble.

There were a number of tablets commemorating those who had served in the Guards, including one to George Whyte Melville, 'Soldier, Sportsman, Author', and a marble medallion of the Duke of Wellington. There was much beautiful mosaic work on the reredos and elsewhere. The tattered colours used at the Crimea and Waterloo hung from their staves on the pillars.

The chapel received a direct hit from a flying-bomb on Sunday, 18th June 1944 whilst a service was proceeding. There were about 180 persons present. The bomb brought down the roof, the upper walls, and the massive Doric pillars and portico at the west door. Lieut.-Col. Lord Edward Hay, of the Grenadier Guards, was struck down at the lectern while reading the lesson and many others were killed. The Bishop of Maidstone, Dr. Leslie Owen, was waiting in the sanctuary to preach, and escaped injury.

A fund to restore the chapel has been opened by the Brigade of Guards. Close by is

BUCKINGHAM PALACE

It takes its name from John Sheffield, Duke of Buckingham, who built a house on the site in 1703. George III removed there from St. James's Palace in 1762 and, for the most part, made it his residence. Between 1825 and 1836 it was reconstructed from the designs of John Nash, the work being completed under Edward Blore after George IV's death.

There were no fewer than fourteen 'incidents' at the Palace; three in September 1940 (one bomb went through the king's apartments); one in October 1940; four in November 1940; one in December 1940; one in March 1941; one in April 1941; one in May 1941; and two cases of damage by blast in June 1944. There was a high-explosive bomb on the Royal Mews in November 1940.

Walk 7

Whitehall ★ Trafalgar Square ★ Leicester Square ★ Soho ★
Piccadilly ★ St. James's ★ Hyde Park Corner ★ Bayswater
Road ★ Baker Street ★ Langham Place

WHITEHALL

THE following are the particulars of bombing in Whitehall:

Address	Department	Times damaged
36 Whitehall, S.W.1.	Admiralty	1
36 Whitehall, S.W.1.	Paymaster General	5
Horse Guards, Whitehall, S.W.1.	War Office	5
Dover House, Whitehall, S.W.1.	Scottish Office	4
Treasury Buildings	Treasury, Privy Council, etc.	4
Whitehall, S.W.1.	Home Office	7
„ G.O.W. (S. Block), S.W.1.	Ministry of Health, Air Ministry, etc.	13
55 Whitehall, S.W.1.	Ministry of Agriculture & Fisheries	6
Whitehall, S.W.1.	War Office (main building)	10
Gwydyr House, 65 Whitehall, S.W.1.	Cabinet Offices	7
Montague House, Whitehall, S.W.1.	Ministry of Labour	14
85 Whitehall, S.W.1.	Admiralty, Treasury	4
10 Downing Street, S.W.1	Prime Minister's Residence	3
11 Downing Street, S.W.1	War Cabinet, Chancellor of Exchequer	2
12 Downing Street, S.W.1	Chief Whip's Office	1
Downing Street, S.W.1	Colonial Office	9
Downing Street, S.W.1	Foreign Office	10
King Charles Street	India Office	9
1A Richmond Terrace	Scotland Yard New Building	1
1-8 Richmond Terrace	Cabinet Offices, Air Ministry	10
34-36 Parliament Street	Air Ministry	4
43 Parliament Street	Government Whips' Office	2
44 Parliament Street	Parliament Street Branch Post Office	3
6 Craig's Court, Whitehall	Whitehall Telephone Exchange	1
Whitehall Court (part)	War Office	5
3-8 Whitehall Place	War Office, Admiralty	1
10 Whitehall Place	War Office	2
Banqueting House, Whitehall	Royal United Services Institute	1

I

The ceiling of the last-named building, which was designed by Inigo Jones in 1622, was painted by Paul Rubens in Antwerp in 1630-5. The subject is the Apotheosis of James I. It was removed for safety during the War.

TRAFALGAR SQUARE

There has been little damage. The paw of one of Landseer's lions had to be replaced and there is still a gaping wound in its stomach.

Marks of damage on the west side of the base of the Nelson Column were made by a fire on Armistice Day, 11th November 1918.

NATIONAL GALLERY (north side). It was erected in 1832-8 and enlarged in 1869. There is some slight damage to the east and west ends.

ROYAL EMPIRE SOCIETY (Northumberland Avenue). Materials for this building were brought from almost every part of the Commonwealth. It was hit by a very large bomb and most of the floors were gutted. On the first floor the research room, containing 15,000 volumes of the law library, and the newspaper room, where files of the chief newspapers from all parts of the Empire were kept, were destroyed. The only contents of the council chamber left intact were two marble pillars given by Malta.

By way of Irving Street off Charing Cross Road, which is north of the National Gallery, one reaches

LEICESTER SQUARE

It was laid out much as at present in 1872-4 at the expense of one, Gottheimer, alias Grant, a financial adventurer who received a baronetcy from the King of Italy.

There has been some damage and of the busts only that of William Hogarth remains. Busts of other residents, John Hunter the surgeon, and Sir Joshua Reynolds, have gone. The statue of Shakespeare (1874) has survived.

On the north side of the Square is Coventry Street, and leading out of its north side is Wardour Street.

SOHO

ST. ANNE'S CHURCH, Wardour Street, is in the section which is north of Shaftesbury Avenue. It was built in 1686. 'Its designer's name', wrote Mr. John Summerson, 'is unrecorded, but it is pretty safe to guess that he was one of the many masons whom Wren had been employing in the City. It was a plain galleried church with an apse flanked by square chambers—a strange revival of one of the earliest forms of church architecture.'

The church is very badly damaged but the tower, erected between 1802 and 1806, remains. It has a curious barrel-like construction near the top and this bears the clock.

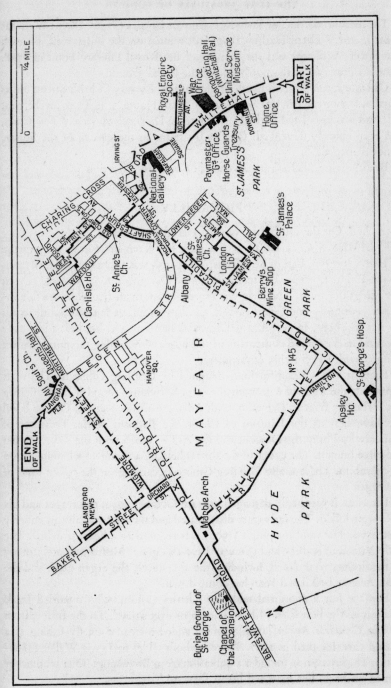

WALK 7. WHITEHALL TO LANGHAM PLACE

The memorial stones of Theodore, King of Corsica (1756), David Williams (1816), and William Hazlitt (1830) still remain on the outer wall, beneath the tower. Williams was the founder of the Royal Literary Fund in 1788. Hazlitt's grave is on the north side of the burial ground.

Old Compton Street is north of the church. By way of Frith Street, on its north side, one can reach Soho Square. Carlisle House, which was on the west side and was associated with Dr. Manette, in Dickens's *A Tale of Two Cities*, has been entirely destroyed. Charles II's statue in the garden of the Square is not damaged.

By following Shaftesbury Avenue in a westerly direction

PICCADILLY

is reached. On the south side, west of Piccadilly Circus is
ST. JAMES'S CHURCH. It was built by Wren in 1680 at the expense of Henry Jermyn, Earl of St. Albans. The parish was taken out of St. Martin-in-the-Fields. Evelyn went to see it on 16th December 1684, and said it was: '. . . elegantly built. The altar was especially adorned, the white marble inclosure curiously and richly carved, the flowers and garlands about the walls by Mr. Gibbons, in wood: a pelican with her young at her breast just over the altar in the carved compartment and border environing the purple velvet fringed with I H S richly embroidered.'

There is also a beautiful font, designed by Grinling Gibbons. The shaft represents the Tree of Life with the serpent twining round it, and offering the forbidden fruit to Eve who, with Adam, stands beneath it. On the bowl are bas-reliefs of the Baptism of Christ, the Baptism of the Treasurer of Candace by Philip the Deacon, and the Ark of Noah with the dove bearing the olive branch. The cover of the font is held by a flying angel and a group of cherubim. There is also Grinling Gibbons's carving on the oaken cases of the organ.

The church was badly damaged on 14th October 1940; the verger and his wife were killed. The ugly spire disappeared and the roof was almost entirely destroyed. The outdoor pulpit (1902) was reduced to a heap of debris. The early Victorian rectory and gateway have also gone. Most fortunately many of the fittings were saved, including the altar-piece, the organ cases, and the font. A huge bell dated 1686 has come down.

There is left a memorial tablet to Charles Cotton, who regarded Izaak Walton as 'the best friend I have known or ever knew'. To the fifth edition of *The Compleat Angler* (1676) Cotton added a treatise on fly-fishing as a second part. He died in 1687. There is also a tablet to Lewis Waller (1860-1915). The inscription includes a quotation from Browning: 'One who never turned his back, but marched breast forward.'

In May 1946, Queen Mary opened here a Garden of Remembrance. The fine-wrought iron gates, with the monogram of George VI were erected in commemoration of his coronation. They were removed for safety during the war. On a neatly constructed board facing the pavement is the following inscription:

The garden of this bomb damaged site was given by the late Viscount Southwood on behalf of the Daily Herald *to commemorate the courage and fortitude of the people of London in the Second World War 1939–45.*

On the opposite side of Piccadilly (at No. 46) is The Albany. It was originally the house of Frederick, Duke of York and Albany, the second son of George III. It was converted into chambers in 1803. There has been some damage.

ST. JAMES'S

On the south side is St. James's Street, and on its east side is St. James's Square where is the

LONDON LIBRARY. Founded in 1841, largely through the instrumentality of Thomas Carlyle, the Library found premises on the present site in 1845. It has lost about 10,000 volumes through bombing—mainly periodicals, biographies, and theological works. There was a direct hit on the west wing and, as a memento of what he described as 'the most exciting night of my life', the librarian intends to preserve a copy of George Adam Smith's *Modern Criticism and Preaching of the Old Testament*, which has a piece of German explosive firmly embedded in its spine. Some of the most precious books had been removed to a place of safety.

On the east side of St. James's Street, alongside Berry's Wine Shop, is an oak-lined passage leading to Pickering Place. This quaint bit of old London has survived the blitz.

ST. JAMES'S PALACE. It dates from 1532 to 1533 but of the original building there remains only the brick gateway, the Presence Chamber or Tapestry Room, and the Chapel Royal.

The Palace was hit by incendiary bombs in March 1941; they caused serious fires. In May several rooms were destroyed by a high-explosive bomb. In February 1944 some windows were blown out by blast: it again suffered from blast when the Guards' Chapel was so badly damaged on 18th June 1944. No damage was done to the older parts of the Palace.

St. James's Park had its share of bombs and one night a courting couple on a seat were killed.

On 25th April 1946, at 7.12 p.m., the German 1,000 lb. 'ticking bomb' which had lain dormant under a footpath in the Park since April 1941, was exploded by a Royal Engineers' bomb disposal squad. Two days before, while some of the men were working in the shaft, the bomb began to tick. As this meant that it might explode at any moment, work was discontinued in the shaft, the park was closed to the public, and warnings were sent to Buckingham Palace and Marlborough House. For two days intermittent ticking could be heard by the bomb-detecting apparatus. The bomb was, however, demolished by two 4-lb. guncotton charges without any 'incident' having occurred. The crater left was 40 ft. wide and 20 ft. deep.

At 145 Piccadilly near

HYDE PARK CORNER

King George VI and Queen Elizabeth lived for about nine years when Duke and Duchess of York. The house (which contains about thirty rooms) has been bombed.

A little farther west, alongside the gate of Hyde Park is

APSLEY HOUSE. It was built by the Adam brothers 1771-8. From 1816 to 1852 it was occupied by the Duke of Wellington. Bombs have caused some damage to the façade.

On the other side of the road, facing east is

ST. GEORGE'S HOSPITAL. It was erected in 1829, from the designs of William Wilkins, the architect of the National Gallery.

It was subjected to three attacks—in January 1941 and in June and July 1944 (from flying-bombs). Some wards were then unable to carry on. There was a pre-war plan to rebuild the hospital.

At the north end of Park Lane (a little to the east of Apsley House and approached by Hamilton Place) is Marble Arch. About three hundred yards west of it, on the north side of

BAYSWATER ROAD

is the ruined

CHAPEL OF ASCENSION. It was erected in 1894 and was the conception of Mrs. Russell Gurney as a memorial to her husband (Member of Parliament for Southampton and Recorder of London), who died in 1878. She proposed to provide a place for rest, prayer and meditation, and wished the walls to be covered with religious paintings. These were executed by Frederick Shields, a native of Hartlepool, whose designs for an illustrated edition of *Pilgrim's Progress* had drawn the attention of Kingsley and Ruskin. Shields said: 'The whole design is to express the eternal purpose of God's redeeming love developing through successive dispensations, Patriarchal, Mosaic and Christian.' Shields finished the last picture in September 1910, and died five months later at the age of seventy-seven.

The chapel has been reduced to a shell, and all the pictures destroyed.

A wooden door to the left leads to an old burial ground of the parish of St. George, Hanover Square. Here, on the left, is the grave of the Rev. Laurence Sterne, the author of *Tristram Shandy*, who died in 1768.

Oxford Street runs east from Marble Arch. Orchard Street on the north leads to

BAKER STREET

There is a big gap on the west side made by bombing, and it seems likely that here stood the house where Conan Doyle placed Sherlock Holmes and his 'Dear Watson'. The late Dr. C. G. Briggs of St. Louis, known in America as 'An eminent Sherlockian authority', thought that the house still existed, and that it was No. 111. This opinion he derived from perusal of the story *The Empty Room* which relates to the year 1894. There we read:

We emerged at last into a small road lined with old gloomy houses which led us into Manchester Street and to Blandford Street. Here he turned swiftly down a narrow passage, passed through a wooden gate into a deserted yard, and then opened with a key the back door of a house.
'Do you know where we are?' he whispered.
'Surely this is Baker Street,' I answered, staring through the dim window.
'Exactly, we are in Camden House, which stands opposite to our own old quarters.'

Blandford Mews may be the passage referred to, but it ends at a point some distance short of No. 111 Baker Street. The latter, which is certainly an old house, probably of the Regency period, has been badly bombed.

Regent's Park is approached by Upper Baker Street. Reference is made elsewhere to a flying-bomb that fell there (see p. 15). Damage has been caused to several of the finely proportioned houses in Park Crescent (in the south-east corner of the Park) designed by John Nash (1812-22). This is the best-known example of 'Regency' London.

By way of Wigmore Street, which is on the east side of Baker Street, at the south end one reaches

LANGHAM PLACE

Here is
ALL SOULS' CHURCH. It was built from the designs of John Nash (1822-4). A circular portico nearly surrounds the circular tower, which is surmounted by a pointed spire, likened to a candle extinguisher. A bomb pierced the roof at the west end.

Close by is
QUEEN'S HALL. It was opened in 1893 with a smoking concert attended by Edward, Prince of Wales. It was highly ornamented and accommodated over 3,000 people. On the second floor there was a smaller hall that held 500. The interior of the hall was gutted by bombs in November 1941.

Greater London

An account of the suburbs in which important historical buildings have been damaged or destroyed

BERMONDSEY

ST. JOHN'S CHURCH (Horselydown). This church, which was erected in 1732, has a tower in the form of a fluted Ionic pillar. It was restored by (Sir) Arthur Blomfield in 1883. The church has been gutted but the tower stands.

BETHNAL GREEN

ST. MATTHEW'S CHURCH (in Church Row), erected in 1740. This church was restored after a fire in 1861. It has been gutted by bombs.

CHELSEA

CHELSEA HOSPITAL. This hospital was built by Wren (1682-92). Later additions were the Infirmary buildings designed by Sir John Soane, architect to the Bank of England.

The building was bombed three times. In October 1940 the east wing of the main building was hit. In April 1941 a para-mine caused extensive damage to the infirmary (the house occupied by Sir Robert Walpole from 1721-42), and amongst thirteen fatal casualties was a pensioner of 101 years named Rattray. In January 1945 more casualties were caused by a rocket which hit the officers' pavilion in Light Horse Court. This had been wrecked by a zeppelin in the previous war. Neither the hall nor the chapel was damaged, but the organist's rooms, once occupied by Dr. Burney, whose grave is in the adjoining cemetery, were destroyed. Grinling Gibbons's statue of Charles II has survived.

CHELSEA OLD CHURCH stands on the river side at the south end of Church Street. The earliest part of this church (the North, or Lawrence Chapel) dated from the early fourteenth century. There were additions at various dates, including the More Chapel (1528); the nave and tower were rebuilt in 1667-74.

There was perhaps no more interesting church in the London area outside the City and therefore its almost total destruction was deplorable. The More Chapel was the only part that survived to any appreciable extent and it will be possible to save its main features *in situ* so that it can be completely reinstated. The arch to the chancel with piers, said to have been carved by Holbein, is intact, and the fourteenth-century timber barrel roof can be rein-stated. The oak reredos, altar and communion rails can be repaired and probably also the pulpit.

The following is the condition of some of the important monuments:

Sir Thomas More. The inscription panel was broken into four pieces and the memorial has been removed.

Sir Robert Stanley. This marble monument (1632) is almost intact. The whole of the upper part, which includes urns, bases, and standing figures, has been removed. This has been done with very slight damage.

Lady Jane Cheyne. The recumbent figure of this monument (1669) was found after the bombing lying on a heap of rubbish to the north of the church. Probably the whole of the memorial can be salvaged and almost entirely restored. A large part of the arch over the tomb and one of the capi-tals have been rescued.

Lady Jane Guildford, Duchess of Northumberland (1555). This altar tomb, with brasses at the back, has now been taken away; it is practically unharmed.

Sir Arthur and Lady Gorges (1625). The inscription on one of the marble tablets concludes: 'When all the Gorges rise heele rise againe.' The tablet has been broken in many places but the brasses are intact.

Richard Gervoise (1563). This has survived, and been taken to St. Luke's, the Parish Church of Chelsea.

Lord Bray (1539). This, the oldest monument in the church, has survived.

Sara Colville (1631). This was in the Lawrence Chapel and represented the deceased rising in her grave clothes from a broken coffin (the stone which formed the base being intentionally cracked), while the clouds in the canopy above are parted to show stars and a dove. There was a similar monument, possibly by the same sculptor, in the Church of St. Giles, Cripplegate (see p. 67). The monument in the Chelsea church has been removed and is intact.

Tablet to *Henry James* (1916). This has survived.

It is feared that the tablet to *William De Morgan* (1917) and that erected by the University women of Crosby Hall in memory of *Margaret Roper* (1505-1544), *Magdalen Herbert* (1568-1627), *Mary Anstell* (1668-1731), and *Elizabeth Blackwell* (1821-1910) have perished.

A 'Vinegar' Bible (1717) one of five chained books is believed to have survived.

Outside the church the monuments to various members of the *Chamber-layne family* (1703) are intact. There still stands also, quite unimpaired, the monument to *Sir Hans Sloane*. The inscription says that he was 'President of the Royal Society and of the College of Physicians' and 'died in the year of our Lord 1753, the 92nd year of his age without the least pain of body and with a conscious serenity of mind'. His collection of books, manuscripts, prints, medals, coins, etc., with the Cottonian and Harleian collections, formed the nucleus of the British Museum. There has also survived the obelisk to *Philip Miller* (1771). He was the first curator of Sloane's Chelsea Physic Garden. A slab close by commemorates *Henry Sampson Woodfall* (1805). He printed the famous *Letters of Junius*. The tablet in memory of *Lord Courtney of Penwith* (his ashes were buried beneath an inscribed stone below) also survived, but it has been removed.

There has been some controversy as to the desirability of rebuilding old Chelsea Church. In *The Times* of 12th June 1946 there appeared a letter, pleading for it, which was signed by Earl Harewood; Lord Esher (Chairman of the Society for the Protection of Ancient Buildings); Alfred Mannings, P.R.I.; Philip Hendy, Director of the National Gallery; A. W. Clapham, President of the Archaeological Institute; Cyril Fox, President of the Society of Antiquaries; Graham Cawbarn, President of the Architectural Association; and John Summerson, Curator of Sir John Soane's museum. The signatories say:

Admittedly, much of the structure has gone, but nearly everything valuable which it contained was salved. Moreover, the main elements of Sir Thomas More's Chapel, with the Holbein capitals, are intact on the Thames-side site, which it would be impious and impertinent for any other building to occupy. In these circumstances, there is every reason for rebuilding the original structure. It was a brick building of absolute simplicity, without a single moulded brick or carved timber. Not a square inch of faked craftsmanship would be involved, nor would the cost be prohibitive. Full records of the Old Church exist, and the monuments could be reinstated in their original relationships.

CROSBY HALL (built in 1466 in Bishopsgate and removed to Chelsea in 1910), which is west of Chelsea Old Church, has sustained very little damage.

There is no serious damage to Carlyle's House, 24 Cheyne Row (east of the Church). There is more damage to the house in which the artist Turner died in 1851 (119 Cheyne Walk).

ST. MARY'S (R.C.) CHURCH (Cadogan Street) was designed by J. F. Bentley in 1879 in the Early English style. It has a wide nave and deep rectangular chancel. There has been damage to the north-west corner.

CLAPHAM

HOLY TRINITY CHURCH (at the north-east corner of the Common). This church was erected in 1776 and thirty years later was attended by Macaulay. It is now the parish church. It has suffered damage, mostly through a rocket bomb in 1945. The tablet on the outside of the south wall in memory of the 'Clapham Sect', as Sydney Smith dubbed Wilberforce and his friends, is intact.

110 NORTH SIDE, the residence from 1914 to 1943 of the Rt. Hon. John Burns, sustained damage by flying-bombs. It has been repaired and converted into six flats.

DEPTFORD

ST. NICHOLAS'S CHURCH (at the north end of Church Street). This parish church has a west tower of late fifteenth- or early sixteenth-century date. The whole of the rest of the church was rebuilt in 1697. It contains a wonderful piece of wood carving, probably by Grinling Gibbons in view of his association with the district. It represents the valley of dry bones (Ezekiel 37). There is also a tablet commemorating the burial in the previous church (in 1593) of Christopher Marlowe, the dramatist. At the gateway there are two skulls carved in stone, known locally as Adam and Eve. The church has been badly damaged but the treasures mentioned here have survived.

DULWICH

DULWICH PICTURE GALLERY (adjoining the old College on the south-west side). This was an earlier collection than the National Gallery, and was started in 1811. One end of the Gallery was demolished in July 1944. All the pictures had been removed to the National Library of Wales (Aberystwyth). Behind it, the seventeenth-century chapel of Dulwich College was damaged by blast.

ELTHAM

ELTHAM PALACE dates back to the fourteenth century. The hall, all that now remains, had been much restored. Part of the roof was burnt in the blitz.

GREENWICH

GREENWICH HOSPITAL. It was erected by instalments between 1664 and 1728, Wren being, for the most part, the architect. It has been five times the object of enemy attacks—one in 1940, one in 1941, two in 1943, and one in 1944. Fairly extensive damage was caused to King Charles Block (1664), and to Queen Anne Block (commenced in 1696). The Queen's House, of a beautiful design by Inigo Jones (1635), which contains the Maritime Museum, was damaged by incendiary bombs. Temporary repairs have been carried out to both buildings.

ST. ALPHAGE'S CHURCH was erected in 1718. This was a large building of Renaissance type, divided into five bays by Doric columns. The architects were Nicholas Hawksmoor and John James. The seventeenth-century tower was recased in 1730.

The church has been gutted. The pulpit and the organ (one of the oldest in England) have been completely destroyed, as also has the Tallis memorial window. The font was badly damaged and almost all the monuments and tablets have been destroyed or injured. There is one happy exception—a brass tablet to General Wolfe, the conqueror of Quebec, who was buried in the church in 1759. The plate has been saved.

HACKNEY

BROOKE HOUSE (Upper Clapton Road). This once appertained to the manor of Kingshold, which came into the hands of Henry VIII in 1538. He is said to have held a court at the manor house, then called Hackney House. In 1547 Edward VI granted it to the Earl of Pembroke. From 1570 to 1583 it belonged to Henry Carey, first Lord Hunsdon. In the latter year Queen Elizabeth held a court here. It is probable that Lord Hunsdon practically rebuilt the house. The next owner was Sir Rowland Hayward, whose monument can be seen to-day in all that remains of the Church of St. Alphage, London Wall. (He and his wife and sixteen children are represented in marble.) He died in 1593 and the house then went to Anthony Redcliffe, one of Hayward's executors. In 1596 it was transferred to Elizabeth, Countess of Oxford, who shared it with her husband and Lady Vaux. Edward de Vere, the 17th Earl of Oxford, died there in 1604. In 1609 the Countess gave up the house. (In the same year Shakespeare's sonnets were published. William Hall, 'the onlie begetter' had been married on 1st August 1608 in the Church of St. Augustine, Hackney. It is probable that Lady Oxford found the manuscript in the course of removal.)

The next owner, Fulke Greville, first Lord Brooke, gave it the name it still bears. In the time of the third Lord Brooke it was visited by Pepys and Evelyn: both the diarists disparage the house, but praise the garden where oranges once used to grow. In course of time there was much alteration but the ceiling remained with the arms of Lord Hunsdon displayed thereon.

It has suffered from bombing but the ceiling is mostly in position, as also is the late seventeenth-century staircase in the southern range. Demolition work has been reduced to a minimum. The buildings of the inner courtyard can be repaired and made even more representative of a large medieval house. It is now the property of the London County Council, and at the time of the outbreak of war was a mental hospital.

ST. JOHN'S CHURCH, a square brick structure with a convex stone portico at each side, was built in 1791-7. There is an elaborate altar-piece, with a stained glass window illustrating the third, fourth, and fifth verses of the first chapter of Genesis. Part of the roof and the stained glass have been destroyed.

HAMMERSMITH

ST. KATHERINE'S CHURCH (Queen Caroline Street). This church was erected in 1923. It is notable as having fittings from the City Church of St. Catherine Coleman (Fenchurch Street) demolished in 1925. They included a seventeenth-century pulpit and an organ loft. There were seventeenth-century monuments and a floor slab.

The church has been severely damaged. The pulpit was destroyed; the organ loft can be repaired.

HAMPSTEAD

KEATS HOUSE (Keats Grove) was three times damaged. The worst 'incident' was caused by a flying-bomb which broke nearly all the windows and badly damaged the ceiling of the large drawing-room added by Miss Eliza Chester in 1838. At the time of writing this room is closed. In July 1943 the house was reopened to the public, though only a few of the usual exhibits were on view, the others being in store at Hampstead Town Hall. On 27th October 1945 the house was formally reopened by John Masefield, the Poet Laureate.

Ken Wood House, the Spaniard's Tavern, and the Parish Church of St. John (1745) have escaped damage.

HIGHGATE

CROMWELL HOUSE (Highgate Hill). Built in 1600, its chief glory is its staircase, with carved figures representing various grades in the army of Cromwell—hence its name. There are also handsome ceilings. It was damaged in 1940 and 1941 and then, having been temporarily repaired, was used as a hospital. It will be restored in due course.

ISLINGTON

The first Parish Church, dedicated to St. Mary, was erected in the middle of the fifteenth century. This was demolished in 1751 and a new one, lacking architectural distinction, was completed by 1754. It has been badly damaged, but the portico is intact. The adjacent statue of Hugh Myddelton, who brought London's water supply from Ware in Hertfordshire in the reign of James I, has not been damaged.

KENNINGTON

ST. MARK'S CHURCH (Kennington Park Road) was erected in 1822-4 and was a 'Waterloo' church (see p. 17). It has an imposing portico. It has been badly damaged. A Church of St. Mark at Barling Point, New South Wales, Australia, sent £924 (in English money: about £1,000 in Australian) to the Archbishop of Canterbury to be assigned to a church of similar dedication in a poor parish. This has been given to St. Mark's, Kennington.

Field Marshal Viscount Montgomery was the son of a former vicar and was bo n at the vicarage, the double-fronted house in Prima Road on the south side of the church.

Close to the church (approached by Harleyford Street) is *KENNINGTON OVAL*, opened in 1845 as the ground of the Surrey County Cricket Club. The tavern and pavilion have sustained damage. A Nazi airman 'bailed' out (the term is appropriate) outside the Hobbs Gates on 15th September 1940.

There was no first-class cricket at the Oval from 22nd August 1939 (the last day of the test match against the West Indians) until 11th May 1946 (Surrey *v.* Indians). This is unprecedented. There was some cricket played during the first European War, notably on August Bank Holiday 1918.

KENSINGTON

KENSINGTON PALACE. This was originally Nottingham House, named after the Earl who occupied a mansion here in the latter part of Charles II's reign. When William III bought it, Wren made many alterations and, later, William Kent made some additions. It has sustained damage, but not of a serious character, and only one of the rooms open to the public was affected. Some of the exhibits were removed for safety.

ST. MARY ABBOT'S CHURCH. This parish church (west of Kensington Palace) was entirely rebuilt in 1869-72 by Sir Gilbert Scott. It is a fine example of modern Gothic, and the steeple is 278 ft. high—the highest on a church in the County of London. The roof was burnt off by incendiary bombs.

NATURAL HISTORY MUSEUM (Cromwell Road, South Kensington). It was erected in 1873-80 from the designs of Alfred Waterhouse, R.A.

The herbarium, in the department of Botany, was set on fire in September 1940. The greater part of the roof and much of the internal woodwork and fittings were destroyed and about 10 per cent of the specimens.

The Shell Gallery was set on fire in October 1940. The roof was destroyed and part of the structure when a high-explosive bomb fell while the fire was in progress.

Damage was done in July 1944 by two flying bombs which fell on the west front of the Museum. Most of the roofs, windows and doors of the main building were damaged by blast. Many of the Nesting Series and British Birds were destroyed or damaged, and considerable damage was done to cabinets containing birds, insects and other specimens.

During the War many incendiary bombs of all kinds fell on the Museum but, except on the above-mentioned occasions, it was possible to prevent them from doing much damage.

The Listener (4th April 1946) related the following incident: 'As a result of air-raid damage to the herbarium of the museum in 1940, the seeds of some plants got damp, including a type of mimosa which had been brought over from China in 1793. In spite of their long sleep of a hundred and forty-seven years in the herbarium the seeds germinated.' This was given on the authority of Dr. Ramsbottom, Keeper of the Museum.

SCIENCE MUSEUM (Exhibition Road). This building had no direct hit, but blast caused damage to windows and to the glass of two large barrel roofs; many show-cases were similarly affected. It was deemed advisable, as a precaution against fire, to strip much of the interior woodwork of the older portions of the premises, the replacement of which by modern structures was long overdue. This, combined with blast damage and deterioration caused by the weather has rendered the galleries useless for exhibition purposes. Work is proceeding as quickly as possible with the recovery of exhibits from evacuation and their arrangement in the available galleries, but the display ultimately on view to the public will be seriously depleted, compared with the pre-War exhibition.

HOLLAND HOUSE. This was designed by John Thorp (1607), but altered in 1638-40, 1704, 1748, 1796, and again in the nineteenth century. The principal staircase belonged to the earliest part of the house and was a good example of the Jacobean period. It was bombed in September and October 1940, when the central block, including the library, was burnt almost to the ground. The upper part of the west wing was also burnt. Some of the panelling and parts of the staircase have been removed from the ruins. The east wing, largely modern, is intact.

OUR LADY OF VICTORIES' (R.C.) CHURCH (Kensington High Street). This church was opened in 1869 and succeeded St. Mary's, Moorfields, in the title of 'Pro-Cathedral'. It is screened from the roadway by houses built in the Early English style. It consists of a nave, two aisles, a deep chancel with domical apse, and two side chapels. It was rich in colour, in paintings and in stained glass. It has been gutted.

LEE

CHRIST CHURCH, Lee Park, was built, in the Early English style, in 1855. The architect was Sir Gilbert Scott. It has been severely damaged.

NEW CROSS

GOLDSMITHS' COLLEGE (Lewisham High Road). This was badly damaged on 29th December 1940. It was, however, found possible to carry on the work.

PANCRAS ROAD

ST. PANCRAS CHURCH. The old church, which was probably built about 1350, was practically rebuilt in 1847-8. It had ceased to be the parish church in 1822. It has been badly blasted.

STEPNEY

ST. GEORGE-IN-THE-EAST CHURCH (Cannon Street Road). This is a large building of Portland stone designed by Nicholas Hawksmoor and erected in 1715-29. There was a fine oak pulpit, and stained glass from designs by Sir Joshua Reynolds. They have all gone. The church has been gutted, but some of the oak saved has been utilized for the panels of a chapel.

STREATHAM

ST. LEONARD'S CHURCH. The first church was probably of the late fifteenth or early sixteenth century—the date of the existing west tower, which is built of flint and limestone rubble with limestone dressings. The rest of the church was rebuilt in 1831. Its predecessor was associated with Dr. Johnson, who attended it when staying at Thrale Place, demolished in 1863. The roof and windows have been severely damaged by blast.

WAPPING

ST. JOHN'S CHURCH (Scandrett Street). This church was built in 1756 and possesses plate given by the first Duke of Marlborough. The tower has been fractured and the body gutted.

ZOOLOGICAL GARDENS (Regent's Park)

THE ZOOLOGICAL SOCIETY was founded in 1826 and the Gardens were opened in 1828. In 1834 the menagerie, which had been in the Tower of London for 600 years, was transferred there.

Mr. G. R. Doubleday, Public Relations Officer of the Society, has furnished the following account of war-time events:

At the outbreak of the War, the dangerous snakes were destroyed. The elephants had been sent to Whipsnade because their house was under reconstruction.

There were absolutely no casualties among any of the livestock. The London Zoo suffered considerable damage from enemy action, receiving fourteen high explosive bombs, some hundreds of incendiaries, one or two oil bombs and one flying bomb which fell in the Gardens; there were eighteen other flying bombs in the immediate vicinity. The only buildings completely destroyed by direct hits were two refreshment bars and the Zebra House. The Camel House and Aquarium received direct hits which caused considerable damage, but did not completely destroy them. Fire bombs badly damaged the roof of the Restaurant and several other buildings. Almost every pane of glass in the Zoo was broken once or twice, in some cases several times, during the war.

The two big tunnels in the Zoo were converted into very fine air-raid shelters and, strange as it seems, in spite of day-raids, etc., there were always visitors in the Gardens. Contrary to expectations, the problem of feeding the Zoo animals was never very great. Our salvation lay in the fact that large quantities of blitzed food unfit for human consumption, were sent to us from all over London.

Outdoor Statues

WHEN a statue of the Prince of Wales, carved in butter, was exhibited at the Wembley Exhibition, Bernard Shaw expressed a wish that many of London's statues might have been made of the same material so that they would have perished in a summer sun. It is remarkable that the more powerful bombs have harried very few of our heroes.

The statue of Queen Elizabeth, outside the Church of St. Dunstan-in-the-West, Fleet Street (its date is 1586) was bricked up. The conjectural statue of Alfred the Great in Trinity Square, Southwark (c. 1395) was left unprotected. Some statues were evacuated. Charles I's went to Lord Rosebery's estate at Mentmore (Bucks.), though not until the middle of 1941, when the worst of the raids were over. Stuart loyalists must have had some misgivings when the statue of the King who

> Nothing common did or mean
> Upon that memorable scene

was hauled away on a common lorry past the scene of his execution. The plinth, carved by Joshua Marshall, was left surrounded by a faked information bureau bearing the inscription 'Closed on Sundays—not open all the week'. The statue of the King returned to London early in 1946. To Mentmore went also the statue of General Gordon from Trafalgar Square, but not until March 1943.

Caius Gabriel Cibber's statue of Charles II remained exposed in Soho Square, but the one in the grounds of Chelsea Hospital, the work of Grinling Gibbons, was bricked up. His statue of James II, which stood in St. James's Park, was sent to the Aldwych-Piccadilly Tube.

William III's statue, from St. James's Square, went to the grounds of Berkhampstead Castle. Another statue of that monarch in the grounds of Kensington Palace was left without protection. It was presented by William II, Emperor of Germany, in 1907, and so has survived two wars. If the inscription had been generally known in the early days of the first European War it might have suffered damage. Queen Anne's statue at Queen Anne's Gate was bricked up, as also was that of George II at Greenwich. George III's was taken from Cockspur Street to Berkhampstead; George IV's was left exposed in Tralfagar Square.

The statue of Oliver Cromwell, presented by Lord Rosebery and erected outside the Houses of Parliament in 1899, was neither removed nor covered. Some might be disposed to cavil at this in view of the care taken over the statue of his king. No doubt the authorities were influenced in the latter case by the consideration that Le Sueur's statue (first erected in 1675) was of fine workmanship and of great historical interest.

To Berkhampstead Castle also went two modern statues: that of Viscount Wolseley from the Horse Guards Parade and the replica of Rodin's 'Burghers of Calais' (given by the sculptor in 1915) from Victoria Tower Gardens.

Sir Henry Irving's statue in Charing Cross Road was bricked up; so also was a bust of Lord Northcliffe outside St. Dunstan's Church, Fleet Street. Apparently all the statues of Queen Victoria were left to their fate—perhaps it was considered that there was an ample supply. The equestrian statue of the Prince Consort in Holborn Circus was not protected in any way, nor were the statues of Edward VII.

The one statue of note that did receive some damage was that of Richard I in Old Palace Yard. This was the work of Baron Marochetti (1860). A bomb bent the uplifted sword of the king and punctured the horse's tail. With the War over, there were requests for repair. Lord Reith divulged in *The Times* the interesting fact that, when he was Commissioner of Works, he had ordained that the sword be left as it was as a symbol, to be explained by a plaque. An inscription was then offered by another reader:

> The battered brand may be
> A token that we
> Were bent but never broken.

A leading article in *The Times* supported the proper repair of, at any rate, the hind quarters of the charger. 'My kingdom for a horse,' cried a later Richard, and the first of his name, if not offering so much, mutely demands one without any undignified holes in its tail. There were two panels round the pedestal. One showed Richard leading Crusaders in an assault upon the gate of Jerusalem; the other, the death-bed of the king. They were slightly damaged and removed for repair.

Eros (which, from 1923-9 was in the Victoria Embankment Gardens) was removed in September 1939 to Cooper's Hill, Englefield Green, where some of the London County Council staff were evacuated. Perhaps the close proximity of the God of Love necessitated the following solemn warning posted by the House Superintendent on 5th September 1941: 'Complaints have been made that much inconvenience and annoyance is caused to residents at Cooper's Hill by the noise arising from the practice of certain members of the staff of taking lady friends to their bedrooms. This practice must cease forthwith.'

The Evacuated Treasures

SOME of the Museum exhibits had to be left to take their chance; they were too large for easy removal and might have been damaged in transit. Amongst these were the Egyptian and Assyrian sculptures at the British Museum and, at the same place, the South Sea Island gods that Dickens thought must have felt at home in the gloom of the Victorian Sabbath. They were protected by blast-walls and sandbags. In some buildings, strong rooms were constructed—at the National Gallery, Tate Gallery, National Portrait Gallery, British Museum, Wallace Collection, London Museum and Victoria and Albert Museum—not for permanent use, but as affording places of temporary storage pending removal.

Eventually most of the pictures from the National Gallery were taken to Manod Quarry, near Blaenau-Festiniog. There, in a vast cave in the mountainside, were constructed chambers, well lighted and given a properly conditioned atmosphere. A road was lowered to leave room for the lorries carrying pictures to pass under a bridge. Bunks were constructed for the guards, there were engineers to attend to the heating and lighting and a telephone and a system of alarms were installed.

It was known in the neighbourhood that the National Gallery Collection was there. Occasionally a picture was brought to the entrance and put on show. Some of the staff brought from London found life in the Welsh valleys rather slow. There was, of course, a village inn but the nearest cinema was over the hills and far away.

To Corsham Quarries, near Bath, were taken exhibits from the British and the Victoria and Albert Museums.

The armour from the Tower of London, and about half of the Wallace Collection from Hertford House, went to Hall Barn, Buckinghamshire. Here, too, went Rubens's famous ceiling from the banqueting hall of old Whitehall Palace. Other treasures from the Tower and from the Wallace Collection went to West Wickham Park, which also received the famous picture by an unknown artist from the Hall of Bridewell, showing Edward VI granting the charter to the hospital (1553). The axe and block from the Tower were sent first to the National Museum of Wales at Cardiff and, after the fall of France, to Caernarvon Castle. Was it feared that, in the event of invasion, they would again be used?

To Mentmore (Lord Rosebery's estate) were sent some portraits from the National Portrait Gallery, the king's coronation coach and the speaker's coach; the organ from the Chapel of St. Peter ad Vincula in the Tower of

London (which formerly served the Royal Chapel, Whitehall); the stalls and bronze grille from Henry VII's Chapel, and the statues and royal tombs, from Westminster Abbey; and the woodwork and Tijou's metal work from St. Paul's Cathedral.

The disused parts of the Aldwych-Piccadilly Tube housed exhibits from the British Museum (including the famous Elgin Marbles) and the London Museum, the wax effigies from Westminster Abbey and pictures from the Tate Gallery.

The invaluable documents in the Public Record Office were provided with various places of refuge, such as Belvoir Castle, Haddon Hall, Lord Onslow's mansion at Clandon, a wing of Shepton Mallet Prison, and the casual ward of Market Harborough. Documents from the City Companies, London parishes, Lambeth Palace, etc., were stored with them. The load for evacuation reached the astonishing figure of 2,000 tons representing 88,000 large packages.

Statues are dealt with under a separate heading.

LONDON TRIVIA, 1941
(With acknowledgments to John Gay)

In this our day, when times are out of joint,
And many gaieties have lost their point,
Some men there be, who in the general gloom,
Will mope, self-pitying, in the sitting-room,
Blaming the car tax and the petrol dole,
Or scheming how to fill the bin with coal.
To these I sing—or would sing if I could,
But that my vocal chords are none too good.
So come, kind Muse, inspire me with the art
To play a strongly stimulating part.
In classic couplets let me write my theme.
(This is the power, though mine the credit seem.)

You citizens of London on the Thames,
Pay heed to these my rhyming apothegms!
Renounce the blues, mix with your fellow-men,
(Should humans emulate the broody hen!)
Forsake the fire; vacate the warm settee;
Ignore the great pontific B.B.C.;
Reach for your shoes and seize a trusty staff,
To show you will not do the thing by half;
Or, if the weather seems to threaten damp,
Provide yourself with somebody's old gamp.
A walk to see the sights I recommend,
Choose you the suburbs, City or West End.
The world of London lies before you spread,
Where millions live and earn their daily bread.
Survey its endless, multifarious views,
Which interest, astonish and amuse.

If cheerful daylight dominates the scene,
Walk on the grass and tread the springy green.
Visit Hyde Park, going from gate to gate,
Where nursemaids air the offspring of the great.
Then take an easy walk along the Mall;
Or peacefully perambulate Whitehall.
Plan to arrive there just exactly when
One hears the mighty voice of great Big Ben.
There's many a statue worth a second peep;
Though others, doubtless, would make angels weep!
Stand and reflect in broad Trafalgar Square.
Notable scenes have been enacted there.
Go farther, to the departmental stores,
With rank and fashion passing through their doors.
See Leicester Square, where 'all the world's a stage'
And actors play their parts from youth to age.

Traverse the Strand, and take that narrow path
Which leads you to the ancient Roman Bath.
Walk on to Fleet Street, hear St. Dunstan's chimes,
And think of Dr. Johnson and his times.
Here is the City boundary, Temple Bar;
And there the Law Courts, where the judges are.
Old Staple Inn you surely must not miss.
Shakespeare himself has often gazed on this.
Proceed from there to famous Doughty Street;
Its pavements worn by Dickens-pilgrims' feet.

OLIVER TWIST was written on this spot.
The site is marked; the world has not forgot.
Then eastward turn your steps. Gaze on St. Paul's;
Or seek out fragments of the Roman walls.
Regard the other churches built by Wren,
One of our nation's very greatest men.
Go far enough to see old London's Tower,
Grim relic of past statecraft and its power.
And ever and anon lift up your eyes
To see those silver captives of the skies.
They serve in the defence of this great City.
We cannot do without them—more's the pity!
In care and resolution do not weaken.
Be sure you cross at a Belisha Beacon.
Ignore this rule, and quickly you may be
No more a walker but a casualty.

And if at night you walk on public ground,
Then mask your torch, with tissue fastened round;
And use it well, pointing a downward ray
To lighten and illuminate your way,
Lest speedy cars, emerging from the gloom,
Precipitate you headlong to the tomb.
The aerial raider searches for a clue.
Be sure he owes not anything to you!

Then when 'tis late, no longer you should roam;
But turn your steps toward your peaceful home.
And when you've reached it, and hung up your hat,
And wiped your shoes on the domestic mat,
Quote this pronouncement to your waiting wife,
THE MAN WHO'S TIRED OF LONDON
     IS TIRED OF LIFE!

O. D. Savage

From *The New Rambler* (organ of the Johnson Society of London)

The carving of a phœnix, over the south portico of St. Paul's Cathedral, by Caius Gabriel Cibber, who was responsible for the sculptures round the base of the Monument. The phœnix, emblem of the Resurrection, was placed over the portico with the word Resurgam below it, at the direction of Wren.

In the beginning of the new works of St. Paul's, an incident was taken notice of by some people as a memorable omen, when the surveyor in person had set out, upon the place, the dimensions of the Great Dome, and fixed upon the centre; a common labourer was ordered to bring a flat stone from the heaps of rubbish (such as should first come to hand), to be laid for a mark and direction to the masons; the stone which was immediately brought and laid down for that purpose, happened to be a piece of gravestone, with nothing remaining of the inscription but with this single word in large capitals:

RESURGAM
(*I shall rise again*)

Parentalia, or memoirs of the Family of the Wrens (1750)

General Index

Adam Street, 17
Adelphi, 11, 17
Air raids, statistics of, 16
Albany Chambers, 123
Albert, Prince, 48, 137
Aldersgate Street, 3, 63, 64
Aldwych, 16
Amen Corner, 36
Amen Court, 37
Apsley House, 124
Arms, College of, 46
Arts, Society of, 17
Ascension, Chapel of, 124
Assay Office, 62
Austin Friars, 50-1

Baker Street, 125
Balham, 13
Bank of England, 49
Bartlett's Buildings, 79
Basinghall Street, 55-6
Bayswater Road, 124
Belle Sauvage Inn, 74
Bishopsgate, 104
Bishopsgate Institute, 104
Blackfriars Road, 85
Bloomsbury, 82-3
Boar's Head Tavern, 91
Borough Market, 41
Bread Street, 39, 40, 61
Brick Court, 23
British Museum, 1, 14, 82-3, 128, 138, 139
Brooke House, Hackney, 130
Buckingham Palace, 9, 118
Bunhill Fields Burial Ground, 105
Byward Street, 94

Cannon Street, 38-40, 86
Cass's Foundation School, Sir John, 99

Central Criminal Court, 32, 37
Chancery Lane, 27
Chapter House Tavern, 36
Charterhouse, 14, 76-7
Cheapside, 13, 14, 16, 52-3, 59-61
Chelsea Hospital, 126
Cheshire Cheese Tavern, 2
Christ's Hospital, 71, 72

CHURCHES:
All Hallows Barking, 14, 93-5
All Hallows, Bread Street, 60, 61
All Hallows, London Wall, 102
All Hallows, Staining, 49, 96, 97, 98
All Hallows the Great, 49, 90
All Hallows the Less, 90
All Souls, Langham Place, 125
Chelsea Old Church, 14, 126-8
Christ Church, Blackfriars, 85-6
Christ Church, Lee, 133
Christ Church, Spitalfields, 104
Christ Church, Victoria Street, 58, 117
Holy Trinity, Clapham, 128
Holy Trinity, Minories, 58, 98-9
Our Lady of Victories, Kensington, 133
St. Alban, Holborn, 80-1
St. Alban, Wood Street, 61
St. Alphage, Greenwich, 129
St. Alphage, London Wall, 102, 130
St. Andrew-by-the-Wardrobe, 46
St. Andrew, Holborn, 14, 49, 78-9
St. Anne and St. Agnes, 63
St. Anne, Soho, 120
St. Antholin, 47
St. Augustine, Watling Street, 37
St. Bartholomew-the-Great, 2, 16, 74
St. Bartholomew-the-Less, 75
St. Benet, Gracechurch Street, 96
St. Benet, Paul's Wharf, 46

Index of Persons